CHEVROLET CORVETTE 1963 to 1967

MusclecarTech

WILLIAM BURT

specialtypress
PUBLISHERS AND WHOLESALERS

Published by

Specialty Press Publishers and Wholesalers
39966 Grand Avenue
North Branch, MN 55056
United States of America
(651) 277-1400 / (800) 895-4585
www.specialtypress.com

Distributed in the UK and Europe by

Midland Publishing
4 Watling Drive
Hinckley LE10 3EY
England
Tel: 01455 233 747 Fax: 01455 233 737
www.midlandcountiessuperstore.com

ISBN-13 978-1-58007-101-7
ISBN-10 1-58007-101-5

Item SP101

Printed in China

Front Cover:
The car that was introduced in 1963 was a great departure from its predecessor. During the previous decade the Corvette received high marks for styling, but low marks for power and handling—the true test of any sports car. The C2 would be the first Corvette that could hold its own with sports cars from any country, thus changing the Corvette's reputation forever.

Inset Left:
Nineteen sixty-seven was the second year that the 427 was available, and there were more versions of the monstrous engine to choose from. The L36 was the introductory level 427 costing $200. It provided the owner with an engine rated at 390 horsepower.

Inset Center:
Buyers flocked to the dealerships in 1963 to pay the relatively high price required to own a Corvette. In 1964, sales would rise slightly to 22,229 units sold. The 50/50 split between coupes and convertibles began to skew in 1964 with 13,925 convertibles being sold against only 8,304 coupes.

Inset Right:
The true teak steering wheel option was discontinued, so it was back to the plastic woodgrained wheel. The wheel was certainly adequate, but paled in comparison to the now extinct optional wheels.

Title Page:
If stately or stylishly aggressive were not enough, the buyer could go all-out and make the '67 downright mean. This coupe has the big-block hood, side pipes, aluminum wheels, and red stripe tires, but has been sheathed in Rally Red paint making it noticeable. Rally Red was carried over from 1965, but there were not as many little red Corvettes that year as one might think. Only 2,341 of the 22,940 cars produced in 1967 were Rally Red, making it the fourth most popular color.

Back Cover Top:
The big-block hood was actually a modified base hood with the scoop added. The scoop on the big-block hood was not functional and actually added drag, but it was worth it visually. It was a perfect visual reminder, or warning, that something nasty was under the hood.

Back Cover Center:
The L36 had 40 more horsepower than the 350 horsepower of the hottest small-block motor, but it added a couple hundred pounds. As a result, the cars were quite similar in acceleration and the small-block car actually handled a bit better.

Back Cover Bottom:
The side "gills" behind the fenders introduced in 1965 were continued in 1966. It would be their last year as '67 brought a new design. These side features are the quickest way to nail a C2 down as being a '65 or '66.

CHEVROLET CORVETTE
1963 to 1967

TABLE OF CONTENTS

I was about nine when I saw my first Funny Car and Top Fuel race on television (damn few races were televised in those days). Within an hour I was at the top of Crestview Road, a wicked hill that ascended Henry Mountain, three blocks long and steep. Under me was my trusty spider bike (red and yellow starburst paint, banana seat, and slick rear tire) and tucked in behind, on the back of the banana seat, was a tight red coil of homemade parachute made from an old sheet. At the bottom of the hill, running somewhere in the vicinity of 275 miles per hour, I deployed the parachute. The chute immediately slowed the bike to five miles per hour, but I was only slowed to 274. I was launched over the monkey bars for an up close and personal "meet the road" experience.

Not much later I later bought a Honda Trail 50 from the kid up the street for $50 and put 834,473 miles on it in the backyard and at a friend's farm before outgrowing it. So began my association with powered vehicles. I have always been a moto-maniac, never focusing on one brand, only on what I liked and wanted at the time. I have owned cars made by Chevrolet, Buick, Oldsmobile, Pontiac, Ford, Dodge, Jeep, Datsun/Nissan, Mitsubishi, Mazda, Toyota, and BMW (an old 1972 2002 that I still miss). Models have included Corvette, Camaro, Mustang, 280Z, Monte Carlo, Cutlass, and lots of four-wheel-drive stuff. These were supplemented by Suzuki, Yamaha, and Honda motorcycles and dirt bikes (I'm scared of old ladies in Cadillacs).

I didn't grow up in a house with a garage so I had to work out most of the mechanics of things in the back yard with a shop manual and scattered advice. After spending an eternity in the foundry and machining business (which translates to just over a decade), I began writing books in 1995. Over that time I have been fortunate in that many experts have given me their time, helping me put together books on NASCAR, Camaros, Volkswagens, more NASCAR, trucks, and tugboats (Top Fuel engines may be the most impressive to stand by, but planting your feet on the shuddering deck of a 100-foot tugboat in full reverse slowing a full cargo ship makes everything else pale in comparison). Anyway, as long as I can pay the bills by hanging around cars and boats I'll keep plugging along. I hope you enjoy the book.

(Photo by David Dickson)

INTRODUCTION

Before getting to the 1963 through 1967 Corvette Sting Ray (also known as the C2 and the "midyear" Corvettes), it is worth looking at both the status of the American automotive industry in the late 1950s and early 1960s and the Corvette's brief pre-C2 history. Cars really began to change in the 1950s. The rolling fenders that graced cars during the previous decades began to disappear as cars became more streamlined. Chrome and colors became more common and more radical. Engines began to grow in size and increase in both power and efficiency. By 1953, Ike was in the White House, the Korean War was over, and America was well on its way to becoming the worldwide king of the hill. The economy grew as Americans enjoyed the good times. This was the atmosphere in which the first Corvette would become a reality.

During and after the war many servicemen stationed in England were exposed to a few British cars such as the MG and the Jaguar XK 120. The open-air cars were like nothing that the sedan-oriented American auto manufacturers produced. In the late 1940s much of Jaguar's production XK 120s went to buyers in the United States. Cars manufactured by MG, Austin-Healey, and Triumph accompanied them. And while many American companies were enjoying the after-war economic boom, Chevrolet was not one of them. Chevrolet sales dropped dramatically in the late 1940s and early 1950s. Their designs were not considered cutting edge and were not catching the attention of buyers. Things had to change.

A key player in events was Harley Earl. General Motors hired Earl in 1927 when Cadillac bought his family automotive business. It would turn out to be a monumental moment in General Motors history. Earl's accomplishments in the automotive world are many and far too long to list here, but he was a huge factor in Chevrolet's turnaround and the Corvette's creation. Earl grew up working in his father's custom car shop and was hired by General Motors to head up its Art and Color Section, which was later changed to the Style Section. Earl gained a reputation for organization, design methods, and innovative design work. But Chevrolet's management team was still very conservative. Earl, owner of a Jaguar XK 120, saw all the little foreign sports cars whipping around and became convinced that Chevrolet could produce a better sports car through which it could both make a profit and help change Chevrolet's conservative image.

In 1952 Earl began working with Ed Cole, an engineer who had come to Chevrolet from Cadillac. Both men were interested in developing a sports car. The two went to see a California boat builder who had built a small sports car prototype based on a Jeep chassis. To Earl and Cole, the most interesting thing about the little car was the body, which was made from a relatively new material called GRP (glass-reinforced plastic). The material made it possible to build complex body panels without the expensive tooling required for stamping out metal body panels. Earl and Cole realized that this could be a viable material and manufacturing option for their sports car. They took the idea and ran with it.

A couple of prototype cars were built under the project name "Opel," and when one crashed during testing, the toughness of the GRP body was impressive. The material was very strong. It did not crumple like metal—it dissipated energy very efficiently through a shattering action. The executives at Chevrolet were impressed with the prototype program and desperate to change the company's sluggish image. Chevrolet approved the Opel team to produce a show car for the Motorama car show. Reaction to the show car was good and approval for the Chevrolet sports car would become a reality for the 1953 sales year. This gave the team little time to get it into production. The Opel tag was dropped in favor of the name "Corvette," which was a small, fast, maneuverable warship. Unfortunately, the car itself was not a staggering performance platform.

The car consisted of a GRP body mounted on a chassis with a box design and weighed in at a little over 2,800 pounds. The wheelbase had the same 102-inch length as the Jaguar XK 120. The front-engine rear-drive was not perfectly balanced, but waas close, with 53 percent of the weight carried by the front tires and 47 percent carried by the rear. The front suspension was wishbone-type control arms with coil springs and a sway bar. The rear had a solid axle with leaf springs. Braking was accomplished with 11-inch drums on all four corners. Inside, the two-seat interior had a European flair with simple, but reasonable, elegant appointments.

The most glaring shortcoming of the first Corvette was the powertrain. Engine choices for the Corvette team were slim and the only Chevy engine that would fit in the car was a 235-ci straight-six truck engine that had been around since before the war. The little engine put out 115 horsepower at 4,500 rpm and produced 204 ft-lbs of torque at 2,000 rpm. The Corvette team bumped up the compression (from 7.5:1 to 8.0:1), changed the cam, modified the valvetrain, and added three single barrel sidedraft carburetors. This bumped the engine's performance up to 150 hp at 4,500 rpm and 223 ft-lbs of torque at 2,400 rpm. This was better but still not good. The engine would carry the name "Blue Flame," but no one was fooled. The car was underpowered and the fact that the only transmission choice was the two-speed Powerglide compounded the deficiency. The pressure under which the team worked was reflected in the 1953 production numbers. The Corvette bacame available to dealers in July of 1953 (the first Corvette came off of the assembly line on June 30) and only 300 1953 Corvettes were produced. Buyers could choose any color scheme they wanted as long as it was white with a red interior. The appearance of the car would remain much the same from 1953 to 1955.

A man named Zora Arkus-Duntov would initiate many of the changes. Chevrolet hired Duntov in early 1953 and his addition to the Corvette team was perhaps the most important event in Corvette history. Duntov was born in Belgium and was racing motorcycles by his late teens. Driven by his parents' fear of two wheelers, he switched to racing cars. He and his family got out of Europe just before Germany conquered Western Europe and settled in New York. Zora and his brother soon opened a parts manufacturing and supply business. Duntov came across the Corvette prototype at the Motorama show in 1953. He was quite taken with the styling, but very disappointed in the car's mechanical capabilities. He was moved to action and wrote a letter to Ed Cole explaining his thoughts. He also included some technical methods to evaluate the car's top speed. When Cole received the letter he was so impressed that ended up hiring him. Duntov would become the most revered man in Corvette history. He brought both expertise and passion to the program and upon his hiring went to work fixing problems on the first model.

In 1954 St. Louis became the home to Corvette production and

changes to the Corvette slowly began to take shape. The only options available on the 1953 model were a heater and an AM radio. For 1954, Chevrolet added turn signals, whitewalls, courtesy lights, a windshield washer system, and a parking brake alarm. While Polo White was still by far the most common color, cars were now available in Pennant Blue, Sportsman Red, and black. A beige interior was also added to the lineup. Chevy hoped to produce 10,000 Corvettes in 1954, but production only reached 3,640. In 1955 there were a couple of very significant changes to the mechanics of the Corvette. A V-8 was first put in a Corvette with the new 265-ci engine putting out just under 200 horsepower. The second change was the availablity of a three-speed transmission. In 1955 Duntov took a prototype Corvette with a V-8 engine and ran the "Measured Mile" at Daytona Beach at 150 miles per hour.

Performance was finally taking root in the Corvette. Copper and Gold were added to the color choices, meaning the 1955 Corvette was available in five exterior and four interior colors. But production and sales of the 1955 were miserable with only 700 cars being sold. Neither of the two benefits imagined for the Corvette program had taken shape. The car was not making money and the image boost had not materialized. In fact, the project was losing heaping wads of money and the under-powering of the car had produced a detrimental attitude with the public. But circumstances would again align for the continuation of the Corvette. While some at Chevrolet thought the Corvette was a waste of time and money, the project still had some influential support at the top. Much of this support was driven by the fact that Ford debuted its two-seat Thunderbird in 1954 and had far less trouble selling the T-Bird than Chevy had selling the Corvette. The market was there and Ford was kicking butt. Any serious threat of the Corvette program ending disappeared.

Duntov's influence became much more evident in the 1956 Corvette, which underwent a significant redesign. Only the instrument panel

remained the same. The first thing buyers noticed was the redesigned body, which had much more pronounced arches in both front and rear. The sides of the car were highlighted with a sculpted cove, which became even more noticeable with the new two-tone paint option. Other notable improvements were the addition of exterior door handles, door locks, roll-up windows, new headlights, and seatbelts. Options also expanded. Body and interior options now included a removable factory hardtop, power windows, and a powered folding top. Along with the new body came more performance. The base engine became a 210-hp 265-ci V-8. Performance options included a high lift camshaft, a 3.27:1 rear gear, and a 225-hp version of the 265-ci engine, which had dual four-barrel carburetors. The sales numbers for 1956 reflected the positive changes. Sales were up to over 3,465 units. This was far short of where Chevrolet wanted the car to be, but it was an improvement. Things were about to get even better. Zora Arkus-Duntov officially became chief of Corvette production in 1957.

Many in the program were saying, "wait 'till next year" and they were right. In 1957 fuel injection and four-speed transmissions became available. A new Chevrolet V-8 replaced the 265-ci powerplant. The engine had a 283-ci displacement and put out about 220 horsepower. It had no less than six option codes for variants of the engine. These included two versions with dual four barrels and four models with fuel injection. Horsepower on the optional engines ranged from 245 horsepower, all the way to 283 horsepower for the fuel-injected engine (one horsepower for every cubic inch). The fuel-injected engines could be temperamental, but when in tune they were screamers.

Duntov and Chevrolet did not stop with what was under the hood. The standard transmission was a three-speed manual, but a four-speed was optional (as well as the Powerglide). Gear options allowed buyers to upgrade to ratios of 3.70:1, 4.11:1, or 4.56:1. A heavy-duty racing suspension was available, as well as bigger and wider wheels. Nineteen fifty-seven was a very significant year. With Duntov at the helm, the Corvette became a car that was considered by the sports car world as a serious contender. It was also a year that his performance-means-sales theory was proven correct. When more performance options were added, the sales of the car almost doubled—6,339 cars were produced. Nineteen fifty-eight included a major facelift to the body, instrument panel, and interior. Color choices for the body and interior also continued to expand with eight exterior and three interior colors available in 1958.

The base engine was up to 283 horsepower and the option list still featured upgrades with the most powerful fuel-injected engine rated at 290 horsepower. Duntov's serious commitment to performance could be seen with the car's new 160-mph speedometer. Although Chevrolet was about to end factory support for racing, Duntov was able to enter two Corvettes in the Sebring Endurance Grand Prix. In 1958, Zora Arkus-Duntov himself, in a Corvette SS, hit 183 mph on the GM proving grounds in Phoenix, Arizona. Sales continued to grow, topping out at 9,168 cars, enough for the Corvette to finally turn a profit. Nineteen fifty-nine saw

minor changes to the car and sales grew slightly. A few changes came again in 1960, but the Corvette got a boost when *Route 66*, a show about a couple of guys' adventures while cruising in their 1960 Corvette, became popular. For the first time sales went over the 10,000-unit mark. In 1961 the Corvette received another significant facelift. The toothy look of the front grille was gone and the rear was much less rounded. It featured the four-taillight arrangement, which would become a Corvette tradition. The interior gained some room when the transmission tunnel's width was trimmed.

Sales were still in the 10,000-unit range but were about to step up. Chevrolet sold over 14,000 Corvettes in 1962, requiring the factory to add a second shift. A big change that helped drive sales was the 283 being replaced with the new 327-ci V-8. This bumped the base engine's output to 250 horsepower. The engine was also available in a 300-hp carbureted version and a fuel-injected model that was rated at an impressive 360 horsepower. The dual carburetor setup was discontinued, as was the painted side cove. As the 1960s began, the Corvette team was finally seeing great success, but they could not rest on their laurels. In fact, they were hard at

work on an all-new design. With Duntov firmly at the helm and confident with his backing, the Corvette took the next step. Sales had increased as performance was increased on the current platform. This was an important fact in determining how Duntov guided the effort for the all-new Corvette. Two more personalities were added to the recipe that baked the C2—Larry Shinoda and Bill Mitchell.

Larry Shinoda was kicked out of design school for attitude problems, went to Ford for a year, then to Packard, then helped build a car that won the Indianapolis 500. General Motors then hired him in 1956. He worked on the Sting Ray Racer for Bill Mitchell, who had purchased the prototype car from General Motors. This prototype racer became the base for the 1963 Sting Ray. Bill Mitchell worked with Harley Earl in GM's design department for many years and took over after Earl retired in the late 1950s. Like Earl and Duntov, he absolutely loved cars. Mitchell, Duntov, and Shinoda were responsible for the C2 design. Between them they designed and built a car that was radically different from its predecessor. In doing so they produced the most coveted and valuable Corvettes in existence.

1963 Corvette Convertible

CHAPTER
1
1963 CORVETTE

When the C2 first made its appearance in 1963 it was obvious that the engineers had cut many of the ties to the past. With the exception of engine configuration and a few interior concepts, the new Corvette certainly had its own identity. No one would mistake any Corvette produced in 1962, or earlier, for a 1963 model. The C2 was its own creature in both styling and performance. Upon close examination, the informed buyer saw that the car was not just different—it was different and progressive. Almost every element of the car had been redesigned or refined, and done so with a desire to improve—not just to change. There were major advances to the chassis, suspension, body, interior, and drivetrain. While styling is always subjective, it is difficult to argue that changes to any of the other areas were not a vast improvement.

CHASSIS AND BODY

The most striking new features of the C2 were never noticed by many of its original owners—the frame and chassis. The design team started with a clean slate when designing the 1963 chassis, and the fact that there were racers in the bunch is evident in the undercarriage design. Like its predecessors, the C2 had a full frame with the body bolted on—but the frame under the C2 was quite different from its predecessors. The chassis still had two longitudinal frame rails that were similar to previous Corvettes, but the frame rails on the C2 were tied togeth-

The 1963 Corvette coupe became known as the "Split Window." Only 10,594 coupes were produced in 1963 and those that survive demand some of the highest prices in the vintage Corvette market.

The Corvette did not enter a market as much as it created a market. America was the land of sedans and did not have a worldwide reputation as a sports car country. The Corvette was America's only mass-produced sports car from the early 1950s to the present, thus having a mystique all of its own. The Corvette was in the dreams of little boys and grown men all across the country.

The car introduced in 1963 was a great departure from its predecessor. During the previous decade the Corvette received high marks for styling, but low marks for power and handling—the true test of any sports car. The C2 became the first Corvette that could hold its own with sports cars from any country, thus changing the Corvette's reputation forever.

The coupe's rear window design was unique within the C2 production years with its center pillar dividing the rear window into two separate pieces. Duntov and Shinoda argued that the pillar blocked rear vision, as evident in this photo. Chevrolet executive Bill Mitchell demanded the split because he thought that it looked cool. All were right.

This cage included vertical pillars in the front and the rear of the door openings, the windshield frame, and a horizontal support in the rear. On the hardtop model the birdcage included a roof structure that ran across the car above and behind the passenger's head with side braces that ran from the cross-member to the windshield frame. While the cage helped the structural strength of the car it could become a problem, as it was prone to rust as the years rolled by. This new chassis provided a solid base for the body and also assured that when the suspension was mounted it would be to a foundation that would allow for excellent performance.

While improvements to frames are great, the covers of the sales brochures don't feature pictures of frames. For the Corvette to sell in the numbers desired, it had to excel in styling as well as performance. To create the body, Larry Shinoda and company went with simplicity, relying on long arcs and some relatively straight lines. Besides the new styling, the big news in 1963 was the introduction of the coupe, or hardtop, Corvette. Before 1963 the Corvette had only been available in convertible form with a detachable hardtop as an option, but beginning in 1963 buyers could opt for a permanent cover.

er quite differently. The previous frame rails were connected with four main crossmember elements. The front and rear crossmembers were mounted perpendicular to the frame rails while the crossmembers located mid-frame were mounted at an angle to the frame rails, forming an "X" shape. The design was adequate for the lower performance Corvette but was not adequate for the high performance Zora Duntov had in mind. The new C2 chassis had five crossmembers and all were mounted perpendicular to the frame rails, creating box-type arrangements down the length of the chassis. This change meant that the new chassis was not only stronger and about 50 percent stiffer than its predecessor, but was also over 200 pounds lighter. The new frame was 145.75 inches in length. In the front the frame was 32.8125 inches wide when measured from the outside edges of the frame rails. In the rear, the width, measured in the same manner, was 45.625 inches. The wheelbase of the new frame was 4 inches shorter than its predecessor, measuring in at 98 inches. When the body was mounted to the frame the new design pushed the cockpit as far back as possible making the 1963 Corvette's weight distribution about 51 percent in the front and 49 percent in the rear. While the C2 Corvette looked "nose heavy," in actuality it was pretty balanced.

The new design also allowed the car to be lower than its predecessor which further enhanced handling. The center of gravity dropped from 19 inches to 16.5 inches. With one design stroke the C2's creators provided a chassis that improved both handling and acceleration. To strengthen the union of the chassis and body, and to add rigidity, the frame was supplemented with a steel "birdcage," which enclosed the passenger's compartment.

The convertible top greatly changed the look of the C2. The roof ended much more abruptly than on the coupes—the long tapering roof was not possible in canvas.

Although it didn't have the graceful roof of the coupe, the convertible did have an expansive rear deck that looked great with the top up or down.

Dimensionally, the new body was shorter, narrower, and lower than the 1962 Corvette. The 1963's body measured in at 175.1 inches long—a little over a 2-inch drop. The 69.6-inch width was almost an inch narrower, and the 49.8-inch height was a drop of about .75 inch. The car also lost a little weight. The 1963 weighed in at 3,015 pounds, give or take depending on options. This was down about 50 pounds from the 1962 model. But it wasn't the body's size that was so startling—it was the shape. While each line of the design was soft, gentle, and pleasing, when they were added up the car stank of aggression. Maybe the design school that ran off Shinoda was right—the car he designed definitely looked like it had an attitude. The previous Corvette's styling was built with smooth curves and soft lines (which were very reminiscent of certain Jaguars' lines). The 1963 Corvette was like nothing the country had ever seen, but the specter of Jaguar was still hovering. Their new E-Type was also significantly flattened out with a long hood.

When assembly was complete, the body section of the car in front of the windshield was essentially one piece (less the hood). The nose of the car came to a distinct point, anchored on a straight horizontal bodyline that ran from side to side. The hood profile rounded down to this line and the underneath of this arc was complemented as the profile of the front valence arced back. In the front, one of the most noticeable things was the lack of headlights. When not in use the headlights rolled back and a body panel that matched the front of the car rolled forward.

The headlights were powered by electric motors activated by a switch on the dash. Below the front edge of the car was a large intake area covered with a chrome grille that featured bold horizontal elements.

In front of the intake each side had an individual bumper, which ran under the headlight assemblies before turning down on the inside and back at the fenders. The days of the five-mile-an-hour safety bumper were still a decade away, so while the bumpers were attractive, they could not actually withstand very much bumping. As the bumpers ended on the outside they accented the new fenders. The fenders featured a continuation of the "front edge" bodyline down the sides and bulged both outward and upward.

Behind the front tire well were two distinct coves stacked one above the other. At the rear of the fenders the one-piece body panel continued inward, forming the cowl area in front of the windshield. This area was slotted for air intake with 25 slots per side. The windshield wipers were mounted with the drive post to the outside on both the left and right sides. The posts came up through the outward side slotted intakes with the washer nozzle mounted to the outside. The small nozzle had a chrome finish, as did the wiper arms. With their outboard posts, the wipers articulated symmetrically, which was much more European. The Corvette's new hood shape was relatively flat. Rising in the center was a pronounced bulge, which tapered to a point in the front.

Each side of the bulge had recesses which featured grille inserts. When the car was being designed the grilles were meant to cover functional vents to allow good airflow to the engine. When tested, the vents actually exhausted hot air. The air was then picked up in the slots in front of the windshield, which were used to supply air to the interior. Since hot engine-flavored air in the cockpit turned out to be not so desirable, the decision was made to use fake grilles, which were completely closed.

The hood was hinged at the front and retained in the upright position by a sliding support located in the front right. The support locked the hood in the upright position. To close the hood the slide had to be released. This was accomplished by lifting the rear of the hood an inch or so before lowering. The untrained oil checker found out that if the hood was forcibly

From front to rear the 1963 Corvette was new—as in new chassis, new body, new suspension, and new interior. Just a few years earlier the Corvette had been in peril of being discontinued. The C2 would sell in numbers that far exceeded those of the car's first decade.

The design of the C2 used long arcs and straight lines accented with peaks and points. When added together, the simple design elements created a perfect blend of grace and aggression.

While the C2 looked nose heavy, it wasn't. The engine and passenger compartments were pushed to the rear as much as possible. This put 51 percent of the car's weight on the front tires and 49 percent on the rear.

pushed down before the support was released, the hood would crack at best and break at worst. The underside of the hood was finished in black paint with the body color wrapping around the perimeter.

As mentioned before, there were two body-style choices in 1963. For the first time the roof actually became a feature of some Corvettes. The new coupe's roof was slightly domed and tapered front to rear into the deck lid. As it moved to the rear it also tapered from side to side, causing the back of the roof to come to a sharp point at the rear of the deck lid. On the top center of the roof, a low "spine" was also added. The resulting look really did resemble the back of a stingray. It is said that designer Larry Shinoda did not care for the spine down the center of the car, but Bill Mitchell did and so that's the way it was. The same decision-making process applied when deciding on the first permanent rear window in Corvette history. The 1963 would always be unique (and years later more valuable) because of its rear window design. The final design, which had the support of Bill Mitchell, featured a post that bisected the rear glass in the center creating the need for two pieces of glass. Neither Duntov nor Shinoda liked the post, arguing that its only function was to decrease rear-view vision. Bill Mitchell again won the argument and the "split window" was created. When the split was later dropped, some 1963s had the post removed and were fitted with a later-model one-piece rear window. These cars were modified long before the

The sharp nose was achievable through a design that made use of hideaway headlights. When the lights are not needed they are not seen, and the back of their housing becomes a part of the body.

The entire light housing rotated back to reveal dual lights on each side. With the lights deployed the look of the front end changed dramatically. As one owner said, "The car looks much friendlier—like it's in a better mood." The bezel surrounding the headlights was made of fiberglass on the 1963 model. The material was changed to pot metal during the 1964 production run.

A grille with horizontal elements was recessed in the front of the '63 behind the bumpers. It was highlighted in chrome and had cutouts where the bumper brackets passed through.

Up front the C2's nose came to a distinct point. Behind the chrome bumpers was a slotted grille with chrome highlights. The bumper arrangement featured separate left and right side pieces.

Each of the front bumpers wound its way from the fender, across the front, and down. The bumpers were easily marred by a low-speed impact and offered little protection in high-speed impacts, but they looked great.

The bumpers were mounted via hidden bolts and brackets. The bottom center mounts extended back and under the car and were connected to the chassis via brackets.

Aft of the hood were slotted air intakes and the windshield wipers. All Corvettes came with a windshield washer system. The nozzle used to spray the cleaning fluid was located next to the windshield wiper post. The sloped windshield was framed with thick brightwork.

split window Corvettes became so valuable, prompting the rear glass to later be re-refitted back to the original.

While about half of the buyers in 1963 chose the new hardtop, the other half stayed with the convertible. The soft top changed the roofline dramatically from the coupe. It was not practical to try matching the hardtop's long tapering profile, so the ragtop curved downward much more dramatically, joining the deck lid much further forward.

The soft top was made of canvas stretched on a steel frame. Dropping the top was a clean and easy process. The first step was to release the clasps at the rear base of the roof. The rear of the roof was then tilted forward so the front of the deck lid, which was the roof's storage cover, could be released. Then the cover could be raised. The clasps on each side of the front of the roof were then released. Once this was done the roof was folded back and covered with the deck lid door and thus completely hidden. This arrangement eliminated the need for a roof cover and made the car look like a true roadster, built with no top. The only drawback was that with the roof down, the precious little storage space behind the rear seats was further reduced. Chevrolet did offer a removable hardtop to mate to the convertible, which is described in the following section on body options.

The doors of the Corvette varied depending on the choice of roof. The doors were truly a work of art on the hardtop. The door windows were completely surrounded by a thick window frame. This frame was recessed inwardly into the roofline, which not only looked stylish in a spaceship kind of way, but also made entering and exiting the low-slung car a bit easier. On convertibles, the doors were essentially the same but without the frame around the window. Both doors featured a main window and a triangular vent window forward. The vent window was framed with chrome trim and rubber gaskets. The Corvette's door handles were a "U"-shaped type with a button to release the latch. The keyhole was located in a circular fitting just below the push button. The 1963 doors had a round driver's side rear-view mirror mounted on a gracefully tapered post. Both mirror and post were finished in chrome and the back of the mirror featured an imprint of the Chevrolet Bowtie. Below the door the car had slotted rocker covers. The rocker covers had a "finned" appearance with the ridges finished in chrome and the recesses painted black.

The rear lines of the car were basically a continuation of those introduced in 1961. When viewed as a whole, the rear of both the hardtop and the convertible had a marine look. The rear of the roof tapered vertically and horizontally as it crossed the deck

The new Corvette's hood was relatively flat with a long, narrow bulge that tapered to a point. On each side of the hood a grille was attached into a recessed area. The grilles were designed to be used to intake air to the engine, but the guys at the factory could never make them work during preproduction testing. As a result the grilles were made as a solid piece and were ornamental only.

The problems with the now non-functional grilles continued after production started. At times they were known to fly out when the car was at speed. A small hole was drilled in the hood at the forward part of the recess to allow water to drain.

The "spine" rising from the center of the roof was carried through the rear window area on the center post. As a result of the design two pieces of glass, two sets of trim, and two installations were needed during production. The elimination of the rear split after 1963 saved money and cleared up rear vision.

lid, resulting in a look that was reminiscent of the old boat tail roadsters or the rear of a speedboat. At the rear of the deck lid the body turned down on the same bodyline that ran from the front down along the sides.

Four small, round taillights were recessed in the rear body panel. Each light fixture featured a chrome ring with a conical red lens. The outside lights were running lights and turn signal lights. All four lights acted as brake lights. The gas tank filler was accessed via a door on the rear deck of both the hardtop and convertible. Under the door was a standard filler cap on the tank neck.

The door accessing the gas filler featured a crossed flag emblem. Like the front, the rear featured a two-bumper setup.

The bumpers started toward the rear of the quarter panel area, wrapped around to the rear panel, and turned down, leaving a space in the center for the license plate bracket. The dual bumpers had a relatively interesting (complex) array of brackets attaching them to the chassis. The license plate was surrounded by a chrome fitting and was illuminated by a light mounted above.

In 1963 the factory gave buyers a fairly wide range of color choices—seven color choices were available. The car could be painted Tuxedo Black, Silver Blue, Daytona Blue, Riverside Red, Saddle Tan, Ermine White, or Sebring Silver. Sebring Silver was a special paint and cost an additional $80.70. This charge was highlighted on the option list as number RPO 941.

The pillar behind the door window on the coupe featured two scalloped recessions that complemented those just behind the front wheels.

In 1963 overall sales of the Corvette were split pretty evenly between convertibles and coupes. Convertible sales ended at 10,919. When added to the 10,594 coupes sold, it meant the public snapped up 21,513 total units. This was the highest in the history of the Corvette and was double the sales of just two years before. The convertible top was available in white, black, or beige. For $237, buyers could supplement their soft top with the C07 removable hardtop.

A small triangular vent window complemented the side window on both the convertible and hardtop. Both windows were trimmed with stainless brightwork.

The fenders came to a point in the front and carried a high center arch along the top. A similar arch on the top of the quarter panels complemented this arch. The wheel wells were flattened at the top to add to the streamlined effect. Centered between the tires were the doors, which were truly works of art in the coupes. The window was secured in a rigid frame that was recessed into the roofline. As well as having lovely lines, the doors sealed well and made entry and exit much easier.

The convertible's door was the same as the coupe's door with the exception of the thick window frame.

On convertibles any color could be complemented with either a black, white, or beige top.

BODY OPTIONS

Options that affected the Corvette's body were few. Soft Ray Tinted Glass was available on all of the windows under option code AO1, or on the windshield only under option code AO2. Back-up lamps in the rear were not yet standard equipment, but available under the code T86 and set buyers back $10.80. When added, the back-up lights were placed in the innermost bezels with clear lenses replacing the red lenses. This left only the outer bezel lights to perform the function of running lights, brake lights, and turn signals. In 1963 few were worried about backing up as only 318 cars received the option. Convertible owners who lived in

The coupe's roof tapered down and into the back of the rear deck lid creating one of the most beautiful set of lines in automotive history.

Each side of the rear panel featured two taillights that were used for running lights, brake lights, and turn signals. Hazard lights were not available and back-up lights were a $10.80 option that was only added to 318 cars.

The gas filler was housed under an ornate door on the deck lid of both the coupe and convertible. This door was one of the few items that changed yearly on the C2. The spine that ran down the roof and deck lid of the car is clearly visible in this photo.

Above and right: The rear of the car was adorned with bumpers much like those in the front. They began at the rear of the quarter panel, turned across the back, and then down. A series of brackets under the bumper secured it to the car with the brackets and bolts designed to not be seen unless viewed from below.

colder climates could still reap the benefits of a hard top with the Auxiliary Hardtop. The optional top was listed under the code C07 and cost $236.75. They were quite popular with 5,739 being produced in 1963. The top used the same fittings as the convertible top and made the convertible more theft proof as well as warmer in the winter. The top was attached with the soft top retracted, so once again, owners had little interior room for storage.

INTERIOR

Like the 1963 Corvette's body and chassis, the interior would receive a complete redesign. The result of the designer's effort was a well-blended mixture of two looks—classic European sports car and intergalactic spaceship (by 1965 imaginary intergalactic spaceship standards). When creating the inside of the 1963 Corvette the designers used soft color and hard metal, straight lines and rad-

ical arches, proven systems, and new ideas. At first look the most striking feature was the distinct separation of the passenger and driver stations. The seats were close together, but the designers used the dash and transmission tunnel to create a look of greater separation.

The dash was divided distinctly into driver's side and passenger's side by ditching the idea of a one piece, full-width dash and going with a design that featured separate dashes for passenger and driver. These consisted of large arches at the top, which tapered to the transmission tunnel on the inboard side and centered on each seat. Each arch was topped with a padded dash panel with matching contours.

Under the dash top, recessed a few inches, were the instrument panel and glove box. The area under the driver's arch was quite crowded. The Corvette was now a serious performance machine so the standard car came with a full complement of gauges. The

Plenty of room for two was the essence of the Corvette and Chevrolet made the interior both functional and stylish. In its first year the interior was available in Black, Red, Saddle, Fawn, and Dark Blue.

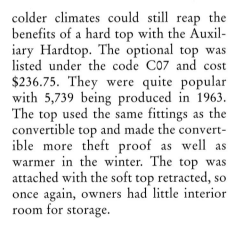

Assembly of the Corvette

When it was time to assemble the body pieces and the "birdcage" chassis pieces, the process used strong bonding agents in place of mechanical devices. These were squeezed onto joining surfaces in much the same manner a chef applies decorative cake icing. The pattern left behind differed from car to car as the compound was squeezed out of the joints when the body was mounted leaving very irregular surfaces. As a result a close inspection of unseen areas can look a bit sloppy. The body was hard mounted onto the frame with large bolts. The A. O. Smith Company of Illinois manufactured the frames for the 1963 Corvettes. Much like a modern NASCAR stock car, the C2's frame was assembled in fixtures, or jigs, which ensured all frames were built within certain tolerances. Without this process each chassis would have variances and would not be consistent with one another. This would have made the addition of the body almost impossible. The frames were painted black and had code numbers painted on them before they were shipped to the assembly plant in St. Louis. These numbers were painted, with stencils, on the passenger's side frame rail. When viewed after assembly they were upside down.

To help eliminate noise and vibration the factory used substantial rubber cushions between the body and frame. The body was shimmed (with the shims above the rubber cushion) in order to properly align each body. After the body was mounted the finishing work began. The automotive world was becoming the pinnacle of mechanized manufacturing, but the finishing department at the Corvette factory was a throwback. All cars were finished with body filler where necessary and then sanded. The first coat of primer was a red oxide type, which had good properties for filling small imperfections. During this process the primary focus was the body seams, which required the most finishing work. After sanding, the car was painted with a coat of gray primer. The body was again sanded and cooked. The body was put in a baking chamber where the bonding agents "glued" the car together and were cured. During this process the bonding agents would often expand, leaving flaws in the finish. If that happened the car was sent back to the body shop for more sanding and primer. The body would repeat the sand/bake process until all of the materials used in the car stabilized and it came out without imperfections.

It was then off to the paint shop where it received two (usually) coats of acrylic lacquer paint. Once applied, the paint job was hand rubbed which brought the lacquer paint to a high gloss. The finishing of the Corvette was a hand-done affair; as a result, the product of the factory was less consistent than today's robotic auto factories. Different people worked on different cars. Each employee differed in both skill and attitude. As a result, the quality of the cars that were produced in the same factory could vary.

The double-hump dash was both futuristic and functional. Both driver and passenger had a separate arched, padded dash as the forward focal point.

gauges and switches were mounted on a plate insert with a textured vinyl surface.

The centerpiece of the arched instrument panel was two large bezels that contained the speedometer on the left and the tachometer to the right. Between the two bezels were the turn signal indicator lights at the top and a trip odometer at the bottom, just above the steering column. Bracketing these is a full complement of engine gauges and switches. Four small bezels contained the temperature gauge, oil pressure gauge, the ammeter, and the fuel gauge. The ammeter and the fuel gauge were mounted on the left side of the instrument panel along with the light switch and wiper switch. The switches were a simple pull type with a chrome finish and black highlights. An additional headlight switch was mounted on the bottom edge of the instrument panel. This slide-type switch opened and closed the headlight assemblies.

The finishes on the gauges changed slightly over the years. In 1963 the gauge faces were flat, painted semi-gloss black. The white lettering on the gauges was and applied to the gauge face with a silk-screening process. In the center of the gauges

The passenger side of the interior was given a twin look that complemented the driver's side perfectly.

The new Corvette was a performance machine and its dash lived up to the task. The car featured a full complement of instrumentation, which shared the limited driver's side dash space with most of the operating switches.

With the top down, the convertible had the look (and at high speed the feel) of an open cockpit airplane. During serious driving, a set of goggles and white silk scarf would not be out of place with this interior.

was a brushed metallic cone concave in shape. The lenses covering the gauges were concave as well. On the right side of the instrument panel were the temperature gauge and oil pressure gauge. The 1963 production began with a 60-lb oil pressure gauge, but an 80-lb unit was used during the second half of production. Mirroring the positions of the left side switches were a cigarette lighter and the ignition switch. The lighter's handle had the same shape as the pull switches. The five-position ignition switch had labels for Accessory, Lock, Off, On, and Start. On the centerline of the lower gauges, the steering column passed through the instrument panel. The column had a small diameter as it exited the instrument panel but was quickly stepped up in size on its way to the steering wheel. The spokes were

The main feature on the left side of the instrument panel was the speedometer that registered an attention-getting 160-mph maximum. An ammeter monitor, the electrical system performance, and the gas gauge accompanied it. The light switch and the wiper switch rounded out the left side.

The right side of the instrument panel housed the tachometer, temperature gauge, and oil pressure gauge. The cigarette lighter and the ignition switch mirrored the positions of the light and wiper switches. The trip odometer was housed between the speedometer and tach just above the steering column.

The turn signal indicators were also between the tach and speedometer. The reset device was a nondescript knob that exited at the bottom of the instrument panel.

Two switches had to be activated to get a C2's lights functioning. The traditional pull-type light switch turned the running lights on in the half-pull position, and the headlights in the full-pull position. The small slide switch mounted at the bottom of the instrument cluster opened and closed the hideaway headlights.

a polished metal surface and the wheel itself was coated with a plastic cover that was color coded to the car's interior. It was well into production before the optional wheel (described later) was offered.

All steering wheels were three-spoke units with the horn button mounted in the center hub. The horn button was circular with a chrome outer rim and a black circular insert. The center insert featured the crossed flag emblem and the outer ring was inscribed with "Chevrolet" at the top and "Corvette" at the bottom in white letters. The arched instrument panel on the driver's side was mirrored with an arched glove box on the passenger's side.

The roomy glove box and was activated by a push button mounted in the top center of the door. The keyhole for the locking mechanism was located in the center of the push button. The 1963 glove box door was made of molded plastic and had a black frame edged with chrome trim. It surrounded a metal insert with a brushed finish. On the lower right side of this insert was an emblem with "Corvette" in chrome script and "Sting Ray" in black block letters. Passengers could rely on a "hold-on bar" that the designers had prudently added to the dash front above the glove box.

Even though it was thin, the area between the driver's and passenger's

dashes was utilized to its fullest. Between the arches the top center of the dash housed the radio speaker.

This was covered with a grille the same color as the car's interior. The center section of the dash then turned down and ran to the transmission tunnel. This center strip of dash was a narrow area. It had a nearly vertical surface and further separated the driver's and passenger's sides. It also gave designers more dash area to mount hardware. This area could be left just about blank by deleting options, or could be quite crowded on accessory heavy cars. On a standard car the area's most prominent feature was a large analog clock, which included a second hand. The face of the clock was

The three-spoke steering wheel featured stainless spokes with a rim that was color matched to the car's interior. The center cap of the wheel featured the crossed flag emblem with the words "Chevrolet Corvette." It also functioned as the horn button.

The center dash piece separated the driver's and passenger's space and was utilized to its fullest. The clock was the front's main feature with the climate control switches just below the clock and above the radio controls.

The passenger's side of the dash featured a relatively large glove box that mirrored the instrument panel's shape and location. The glove box featured a lock that was integral with the release button—especially helpful to convertible owners.

A mesh screen resided on the top center of the dash and covered the radio speaker at the top.

black with white numbers and the 12-hour markings were supplemented with minute marks. Just below the clock on each side were the climate control switches. On base cars this consisted of a fan, heater, and defroster control. The left switch controlled the fan speed by twisting and the air temperature by pulling. The right switch was pulled to change from vent air to defrosting. Below the climate control switches were the switches for the radio, which were quite unique. In order for a radio to fit into the limited space that was available, Chevrolet had to have a custom unit produced. The main body of the radio was turned 90 degrees and mounted vertically.

The section of the radio containing the knobs was relocated into a separate unit mounted directly on top of the main body. The switches for the radio matched the climate control switches and were mounted below them, forming a box pattern. The left-side knob was the volume and tone control and the right-side knob was the tuning dial. The base car came

An ornamental plate surrounded the shifter with the shifter pattern inscribed to the rear. An ashtray with a sliding door was to the right of the shifter. The all-metal finish on the shifter plate was only used in 1963.

A small, thin duct stationed to each side of the center console was part of the climate control system. These hardly noticeable features were another example of the wonderful attention to detail all over the C2.

with an AM radio, which had five pushbutton presets mounted on the right side of the unit. The base of the center strip of dash ended abruptly at the transmission tunnel, which had its own cover. A chrome piece of trim defined the line where the two pieces met.

A flat panel trimmed in chrome covered the transmission tunnel and had an inner surface with a muted metallic finish. The shift lever emerged through the plate on the left side of the top surface, and the right side was reserved for a small ashtray with a nifty sliding top. The area that housed the shifter and ashtray had a brushed aluminum surface. In the center of the plate, behind the shifter, was a shift pattern indicator.

Seats for the 1963 Corvette were pretty basic. The standard seat package consisted of two buckets with black vinyl seat covers. The seat design of the 1963 model was unique. The backrest of the seat tapered as it reached the top and both the backrest and the seat bottom had vertical stitching, dividing them into about a dozen narrow sections. The seats had a front-to-rear adjustment with the locking lever located under the seat bottom at the front. If the interior color was changed from black so was the seat cover as each of the five interior colors available had matching vinyl seat covers.

Another never-before-offered option made an appearance in the 1963 production year—leather seats. The leather seats could be had in any color as long as it was Saddle Tan.

Radio choices were few and all were expensive. Adding an AM only radio (shown here) would set buyers back $138. To purchase a radio that could receive the emerging technology of frequency modulation (FM) would cost buyers $174. This meant that adding an AM radio was more expensive than an optional engine with 90 more horsepower.

Cars with red, black, Dark Blue, or Fawn interiors had vinyl seats that matched the interior color.

The door panels in the 1963 model were a basic non-molded rectangular piece made of vinyl and were also color matched to the car's interior.

The standard panels featured a chrome crank handle to open the main window. A matching but smaller vent window crank was mounted higher and more forward of the main window crank. The inside door latch was a small stylish unit with a simple chrome knob in a slotted fixture on the door panel. The slot was surrounded with a chrome trim piece. The throw of the latch was very short and being so small was quite unobtrusive. A small armrest was mounted towards the rear of the panel and provided a bit of comfort if your body was the right size (the size being

Both seats tilted forward to allow access to the rear storage compartments. The backs of the seats did not lock into position and could fly forward with the passenger and driver during sudden stops.

The bucket seats in the '63 Corvette were unique with their slightly tapering backrests. Stitching was longitudinal, also unique to the '63. The simple seat adjuster was located at the front of the seat bottom.

small). At the rear of the door panel were two circular fixtures. The top was the door lock while the bottom was a dummy that was purely for styling. Along the bottom of the door panel was a strip of carpet that matched the flooring carpet. The door panels were attached with 10 Phillips-head screws. The screws had chrome washers and were visible around the perimeter of the door. The carpeting on the 1963 was 80/20 double-twisted nylon loop cut in multiple flat pieces (as opposed to molded carpets) with jute backing.

The exposed edge of the carpet was stitched with vinyl trim. The area behind the seats differed between the coupe and roadster. When buyers chose the convertible there was little room for storage behind the seats, and much of the room that was available with the top up disappeared when the roof was retracted. Both coupe and convertible did have a couple of storage compartments. One of these was under a removable panel (with a carpet cover) behind the seats, low in the interior. This area housed the jack and provided a bit of extra storage for tools or a decent emergency kit. The jack was a scissor type and finished with gloss black paint. The inside of these compartments were painted with a flat finish that roughly matched the car's interior color. The inside of the lid had the jacking instructions, and on cars equipped with the Positraction option an additional sticker warned the owner not to put the car in gear while on jack stands.

Five interior colors (black, Saddle,

The door panels on the new Corvette were a multi-piece design that would later be replaced with a molded panel. Dual window cranks operated the windows and the small, elegant knob latch opened the door. A piece of carpet that matched the interior's color was added at the bottom of the panel below the window crank. The door lock was at the top rear of the door panel and was accompanied by a dummy twin. This "fake" door lock was removed during the 1964 production year. In '63 the armrest was a separate piece that was bolted on.

The coupe offered a fair amount of storage for a powerful two-seater. The carpet on the '63 consisted of flat pieces cut and fit to the interior. It would be replaced with molded carpet in later years. At night, light was provided throughout the coupe by an overhead dome light.

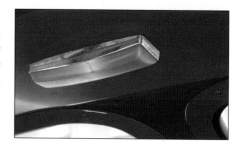

Fawn, red, and Dark Blue) were available in 1963. Availability was limited depending on the exterior color of the car. The black interior was the only one available with any exterior color. Saddle could be installed in cars painted Tuxedo Black, Riverside Red, Saddle Tan, Ermine White, or Sebring Silver. The Red interior came in cars painted Tuxedo Black, Silver Blue, Riverside Red, Saddle Tan, Ermine White, or Sebring Silver. The Fawn interior was only available on cars painted Silver Blue or Daytona Blue, and the Dark Blue interior came in cars painted Ermine White or Sebring Silver.

INTERIOR OPTIONS

Options for the interior of the Corvette also expanded in 1963. Perhaps the biggest news was the availability of air conditioning. Surprisingly, it was a rare option, coming on only 278 cars. The layout of the center strip changed if the car was equipped with air conditioning. A slim vent ran from side to side at the top. Just below the vent and above the clock two additional pull switches were installed. The left-hand switch activated the air and the right-hand switch controlled the temperature. Along with the center dash duct and the ducts aside the console, factory-added ducts ran under the dash and exited to the outside on both driver and passenger side. The A31 Power Window option was continued with the new Corvette and was reasonably priced at $59. Even so, power window equipped cars are rare. Only 3,742 1963 Corvettes were equipped with the system.

For the complete performance enthusiast, or for those who lived in a desert, a $100 credit was offered under RPO code C48 for deleting the heater and defroster. This option was rare with records showing that only 124 buyers ordered their 1963 with a heater delete. By purchasing the car in "heater delete" form, a fair bit of weight was saved by eliminating the heater care, ducting, hoses, and controls. It was an option usually chosen by those who wished to race their Corvette.

Buyers also had a couple of entertainment options for their 1963 Corvette. The cost of the base car did not include a radio as standard equipment, but most Corvettes were shipped radio equipped. Radio technology was far from what it is today, but the Corvette offered what was the top-of-the-line for the times. The first radio choice was the U85 Signal Seeking AM radio. The U85 was the most common Corvette radio, being installed in 11,368 1963s. Electronics were not cheap in 1963 and due to the dash layout the Corvette required a custom radio unit that was not used on any other General Motors product. As a result, the simple push button AM radio cost buyers $138. This made the cheapest radio option more expensive than the most powerful carbureted optional engine. The other radio choice was even more costly. The U69 AM-FM Radio allowed buyers to tune into the relatively new FM technology. The U69 was installed in 9,178 cars and listed at $174. Totaling these numbers shows that of the 21,513 Corvettes produced in 1963 almost 96 percent of them came with a sound system. Another amenity to spruce up the interior was the N34 wood-grained steering wheel. It was made of plastic, not real wood, and few (only 130 people) chose to shell out the $16 required to purchase one. The optional wood-grained steering wheel did not come out until March of 1963 after over 10,000 Corvettes had already left the factory.

ENGINE & DRIVETRAIN

While the body, interior, and suspension were all new for 1963, the Corvette relied on engines that had been developed and introduced during the previous model's reign. In 1963 all Corvette engines were variants of the 327-ci V-8, which first appeared in the 1962 Corvette. The base 327-ci engine for 1963 produced 250 horsepower at 4,400 rpm and 350 ft-lbs of torque at 2,800 rpm. Like all Corvette 327s, the engine had a bore of 4.00 inches and a stroke of 3.25 inches, and the base motor was built with a compression ratio of 10.50:1. Fuel was delivered to the engine via a four-barrel Carter carburetor. The carburetor was topped with a closed air intake with twin snorkel-like intakes that faced forward. The exhaust was piped from the engine through cast iron exhaust manifolds leading into a dual exhaust. Two-inch exhaust pipes carried the mufflers and were mounted under the rear of the car to each side of the spare tire carrier.

While it was the tamest of the 1963 Corvette engines available, the 327 was far better than what was available in the early years of the Corvette. Its power was immense when compared to the engine used a decade before and was significantly better than the 265-ci and 283-ci engines used in the mid to late 1950s and early

The 327 introduced to the Corvette line in 1962 was to be the workhorse of the C2 platform. In 1963, Chevrolet offered four variants of the small-block power plant.

The most common engine found in 1963 was the L75, which added $54 to the base car's price. The engine package also added 50 horsepower over the base 327 and was installed in over 8,000 1963 Corvettes.

The carburetor on the L76 was topped with a semi-open air cleaner complete with chrome housing. The side of the housing had sections cut out to allow adequate airflow to the engine.

The next most popular engine was the L76, a solid-lifter motor that was fed by a four-barrel Carter carburetor. The L76 cost $108 and was in almost 7,000 1963s.

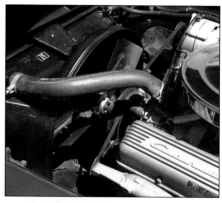

A tight, efficient fan shroud was necessary to keep the Corvette engine cool, but was especially important in the high-compression, high-performance engines.

1960s. Even so, coming across a 1963 Corvette equipped with the base engine is pretty rare, both now and in 1963. Only 3,892 1963 Corvettes were produced without an optional, more powerful engine. The fact that the base engine was only installed in a little over 18 percent of the 1963 Corvettes produced was a testament to Corvette buyers' need for speed. The other 82 percent chose to dine on the engine option list when ordering their cars. In 1963 they could select one of three optional engines. The base engine was finished with Chevrolet Orange covering the block, heads, valve covers, and intake manifold.

Working up the engine list on the basis of horsepower, the first available optional power plant was the L75. A 327-ci unit, the upgrade cost only $53.80 and power was boosted by 50 horsepower. Since displacement was the same in all Corvette engines, the factory had to use performance parts and systems to increase power. Like the base motor, the L75 was built with 10.50:1 compression, but was built to spin faster. The L75 used a Carter four-barrel carburetor that rested on a painted manifold. The air cleaner was the same used on the base engine. Redline for the L75 was 5,500 rpm. All L75s had cast-iron exhaust manifolds, but the exhaust could vary. If the L75 was mated to a manual transmission it had 2-1/2-inch exhaust, while L75s mated to Powerglide automatics had 2-inch exhaust. Chevrolet rated the engine at 300 horsepower at 5,000 rpm and 360 ft-lbs of torque at 3,200 rpm. Visibly the L75 was very similar to the base engine. The only external differences in appearance were the use of a different fuel line (with an inline filter located between the fuel pump and the carburetor) and the engine's decals.

The next step up on the engine list was the L76. By further internal massaging, the 327 Chevrolet was able to spin the engine even faster, creating an additional 90 horsepower over the base engine and 40 over the L75. This meant that the L76 was rated at 340 horsepower at 6,000 rpm, 344 ft-lbs of torque at 4,000 rpm, and redlined at 6,000 rpm. Bumping the compression to 11.25:1 created some of the L76's additional power. The L76 had a different cam arrangement as well. The cam itself was a bit more radical and used mechanical, or solid, lifters in place of the hydraulic lifters used in the base engine and L75. The mechanical lifter engines could be a bit more temperamental, but made for a more efficient valvetrain. The L76 was also topped with an unpainted four-barrel Carter carburetor on an aluminum intake. The air cleaner was a semi-open element with a chrome finish.

The bottom of the oil pan was pretty close to the road. C2s that were, and are, regular drivers most likely have a dented oil pan. The starter, oil filter, and small rear main seal leak are all visible.

By far the most common transmission was the four-speed. In 1963 17,983 C2s were equipped with the optional M20 four-speed (seen here), leaving only 3,540 cars with the standard three-speed or the optional Powerglide automatic.

The L76 was the most powerful carbureted Corvette engine available, but not the most powerful overall. The last engine available on the option list was the L84 fuel-injected 327. The L84 differed greatly from the other engines as the carburetor was scrapped for a Rochester mechanical fuel injection system. Like the L76, the L84 was built with an 11.25:1 compression ratio and used mechanical lifters in the valvetrain. As a result, the engine was able to produce an impressive 1.100917431 horsepower per cubic inch. The factory rated the engine at 360 horsepower at 6,000 rpm and 352 ft-lbs of torque at 4,000 rpm. Like the L76, it redlined at 6,000 rpm. While it was the king of the horsepower, the L84 was the least common of the Corvette engines. The reason for its rarity is twofold. First, it was expensive. At $430.40 the engine meant an investment in an option that represented about 10 percent of the entire base car's cost. The second reason was the reputation (deserved or not) of the finicky-ness of the fuel injection unit.

If the engine was tuned correctly it was a screamer but if not it ran rough (of course the same can be said of a carbureted engine). Even though Chevrolet had sold fuel injection options since the 1950s, it was still newfangled technology for many people in 1963. But those who took the $430.40 plunge were well rewarded—mainly in performance,

The driveshaft fit neatly in a small tunnel and was bracketed by the exhaust pipes (right). All Corvettes came with dual exhaust. The exhaust system began with cast-iron headers that had a better performance design than many stock manifolds (but still not as good as a set of tubular steel headers). The manifolds led to the pipes, which ran to the rear and actually passed through the crossmember under the center of the car. The exhaust pipes entered mufflers that were hung aft, on each side of the spare tire carrier. The exhaust then exited through the rear body panel.

but also in style. Bolted to the top of the engine the fuel injection unit was an attractive element. It had a metal finish with a finned top featuring a crossed-flag emblem. Because of the design, the air cleaner left its traditional position on top of the engine and was relocated to a canister in the left front of the engine compartment. The air was picked up there, run through the filter, and to the engine through an intake tube. All these components were painted black.

As mentioned before, 82 percent of the Corvettes sold in 1963 were sold with an optional engine upgrade. The L75 was the most popular with 8,033 being produced. Next was the L76 at 6,978 and the L84, pricey at $430.40, was installed in only 2,610 Corvettes. Only 3,892, or 18 percent of, 1963 Corvettes left the assembly line with a base engine.

The front suspension of the C2 is quite conventional, consisting of upper and lower control arms, coil springs, and shocks. It was assembled with off-the-shelf Chevrolet parts in order to save money so that the expensive independent rear suspension could be added.

ENGINE OPTIONS

Besides the engines there were a couple of other choices on the option list for the performance enthusiast. The first was the high-capacity fuel tank. To lengthen the time between pit stops, buyers could replace the stock fuel tank with a 36-gallon fuel tank. The option was expensive, costing $202, and took up much of the already limited space in the rear. As a result only 63 Corvettes were known to leave the factory in 1963 with the high capacity tank. Due to space issues the 36-gallon tank was only available when ordering a hardtop. For racers (and street drivers who would risk tickets) the N11 option added a free flow, un-muffled exhaust. Known as the "off-road exhaust," the option added horsepower and while not street legal cost only $38.

DRIVELINE

The performance attitude of the redesigned Corvette continued aft of the engine. The flywheel was protected with a lightweight, alloy bellhousing. The base transmission was a Saginaw three-speed manual shift unit. This three-speed was much like the base engine. While this was the standard transmission, it is the most uncommon gearbox found in the surviving 1963 Corvettes. In the world of Corvettes, transmissions were like engines—the standard was rarely suitable. Less than 1,000 1963s left the factory with the three-speed. Almost 96 percent of the Corvettes produced in 1963 had optional transmissions. The first choice was the M20 wide ratio four-speed, which sufficed as a performance transmission. It was by far the most popular choice and was installed in 17,973 (83.5 percent) of the Corvettes produced in 1963. This was largely due to its being mated with many of the popular performance engines. The M20 cost buyers $188 and was available throughout the Chevrolet line.

The other transmission on the 1963 option list was Chevrolet's Powerglide. The Powerglide was a two-speed automatic and a concession to those who could not or would not drive a manual transmission. The Powerglide cost buyers $199 and was installed on 2,621 (12 percent) of the 1963 Corvettes produced.

Regardless of choice, the transmission was linked to the rear gear by a short driveshaft equipped with universal joints at each end. The rear gear drove short half-shafts, which transferred the power to the rear hub assemblies and then to the tires. The half-shafts were equipped with universal joints at each end. Gear choices in 1963 included a 3.36:1, 3.55:1, 3.70:1, 4.11:1, and a stump-pulling 4.56:1. For those more interested in economy, the gear could also be replaced with a higher ratio 3.08:1 highway gear for a meager $2.20. Only 211 buyers chose to do so, as the highway gear seriously inhibited acceleration. The rear end could be upgraded to a Positraction unit for a little over 40 bucks—and most were. The Positraction option appeared on 17,554 of the 21,513 Corvettes produced in 1963.

SUSPENSION, STEERING & BRAKES

Zora Duntov had to struggle for the 1963 Corvette's suspension to become a reality. The front suspension wasn't a problem. The pain was in the rear. Duntov wanted to move away from a solid rear axle and put an independent rear suspension under the new Corvette. Top management was against it based on one fact—cost. Independent rear suspensions are significantly more expensive to produce than solid axle rear suspensions. Duntov knew that the handling capability of the car would be dramatically increased with his suspension, but the "performance means sales" argument

Most of the C2's steering system is located behind the front tires. The steering gear drives the pitman arm, which moves the center-link from side to side. This in turn moves the idler arms and the steering knuckles. The relatively lightweight Corvette seldom came with the power steering option as it cost more, drained power from the engine, and was not needed by most drivers to turn the small car.

was not enough without a concession by Duntov. To help offset the cost of the rear suspension, Duntov agreed that the 1963 Corvette would have a front suspension that used existing Chevrolet parts. The Corvette team chose front-end parts from the Impala and the new rear suspension was finally approved.

Handling of the new car was greatly increased because of the new rear setup, but was also aided by a chassis and body redesign. The redesign helped drop the Corvette's center of gravity from 19 inches to 16.5. It also meant that the car had a five-inch ground clearance. The weight distribution was 51 percent on the front tires and 49 percent on the rear tires. The Corvette team raised the roll center of the Corvette with the 1963 model. In simple terms, the car's roll center is the line on which the body rolls in the chassis during cornering. A car's roll center is very important to handling—by changing it, the Corvette's designers wanted to keep as much of the Corvette's narrow tires on the road as possible. The new 98-inch wheelbase was 4 inches shorter than previous Corvettes. It had a 56.25-inch front track and a 57-inch rear track.

In 1963 the rear suspension was an area where the Corvette caught up

to some cars and blew past others. With Duntov's insistence that the Corvette have a four-wheel independent suspension, he ensured that the Corvette would be taken very seriously by the sports car world. The independent rear setup was more common on European performance cars, but was a rare commodity in America. Instead of a solid rear axle, the Corvette would use flexible halfshafts (via "U" joints at each end) that ran from the rear gear to the wheel hubs at the back of the trailing arms. The geometry and performance of this suspension were far more advanced than the previous Corvette's solid axle rear suspension. On a solid axle rear suspension, each rear wheel influences the movement of the other. If the left rear wheel moves down (into a pothole), the axle will tilt, tilting the right rear wheel as well. With an independent rear, the right wheel is not influenced as the left side drops and remains vertical. The trailing arms were attached to the frame with a bolt that was shimmed to set the toe of the wheel. In 1963 these shims had the bad habit of moving and were later modified to be kept more secure. The trailing arms were sprung with a traverse-mounted single leaf spring. It is said that Duntov did not like the look of

the suspension, but it worked quite well and was by far the easiest and least expensive way to spring the rear. The standard spring had nine steel leafs. It was bolted under the rear gear in the center and to the trailing arms on the outer ends via strong bolts. Along with the leaf spring the trailing arm was sprung with a black Delco shock absorber.

The front suspension of the Corvette was actually pretty basic with Impala control arms and steering knuckles (linked together with upper and lower ball joints). The ball joints were riveted to the control arms at the factory. A few low-mileage cars still have the rivets in place, but cars that have had the ball joints replaced usually have ball joints mounted with studs and nuts. The control arms (also known as "A" arms or "wishbones") were made of pressed steel and painted black. The geometry of how the parts were mounted was different than how they were mounted on the Impala. The conventional front suspension was sprung with coil springs and shocks. The coil springs were mounted between the frame and the lower control arm. Springs on the first few 1963 Corvettes were a bit weak, and a stiffer, stronger spring was soon introduced. Delco made shocks for the 1963 Corvette and they were painted black. The front suspension was completed with the addition of a 3/4-inch sway bar that linked the chassis to the suspension. The bar's center section was mounted to the frame rails with brackets that contained bushings. The ends of the sway bar were attached to the lower control arm with links, which also had bushings.

A large steering box containing two gears provided steering for the new Sting Ray. The steering shaft ran from the steering wheel, through the column, through the firewall, and to the steering box. The gear had an adjustment point on the top that consisted of an adjustable setscrew secured with a lock nut. When the lock nut was loosened the setscrew could be turned to adjust the lash between the gears. The rotary action of the steering shaft was turned into a lateral motion by means of the Pittman arm. This attached the steering gear to the center

Left: The rear suspension was sprung with a single leaf spring. The back of the trailing arm was the meeting place for the leaf spring, the half-shaft, the radius rod, and the wheels. All of these components came together in a small space.

Right: The C2 began life with drum brakes on all four corners. It was the car's only performance disappointment. Those who own and drive Corvettes with drum brakes have to think further ahead than those with the later disc-brake-equipped Corvettes.

shaft, which is also supported by the idler arm. Adjustable tie rods linked the center shaft to the steering knuckles and thus to the front wheels. The standard steering system for 1963 was a manual, non-powered unit that required a bit of muscle to turn, especially when the car was not moving. But 1963 saw yet another Corvette first. Under the code of N40, Corvette buyers could purchase power steering for a very reasonable $75. Power steering had been around for a while, but to most of the automotive world it was not a necessity and was certainly not a standard feature as it is today. Just over 3,000 Corvettes left the factory with the N40 option. A small, belt-driven hydraulic pump located on the left side of the engine supplied power for the system. The pump supplied the pressure for the system, which was managed with a control valve and a power cylinder. The control unit could sense the way the wheel was turning and would expand or contract the cylinder depending on whether the car was turning left or right. Hydraulic lines with rubber exteriors and crimped fittings ran between the pump, control valve, and cylinder. The system worked well, but as miles accumulated it could develop small leaks.

When it came to the 1963 Corvette brake system, the truth of the matter is that performance fell a bit short.

The car's creators knew this, but they had introduced a car with many changes and the introduction of new systems had to stop somewhere. Both

the Corvette design team and the general public had to wait a couple more years for an adequate way to stop the new, more powerful, car. The 1963 base braking-system remained a non-powered system with drums on all four wheels. A small single master cylinder painted black and capped with a metal lid with a natural finish powered the system. The lid was held in place with a flattened thumbscrew. The metal brake lines ran from the master cylinder into a small hydraulic wheel cylinder on each individual wheel. The cylinders expanded when the master cylinder was engaged and pressed the brake shoes against the machined inner surface of the brake drum. The bottom of the shoes pivoted on an adjustable pin used to adjust the brakes. The wheel cylinders used on the front brakes were a bit bigger than the ones on the rear brakes. The front brakes did almost 60 percent of the braking and the different sized wheel cylinders helped to balance the car under braking. The emergency brake was activated by a reasonably complex cable system that ran under the car.

If there was a major element missing on the 1963 Corvette it would be the brakes, but the buyer could improve the stock brakes a bit. Braking was made easier with the $43 J50 Power Brake option, which added a vacuum chamber to the master cylinder. This chamber assisted the driver in applying pressure to the pedal, but did not change the brakes themselves. The J65 Metallic Brake option did change the brakes. This $38 option replaced

the base brake-shoes with more efficient metallic shoes on all four drums.

Every Corvette shipped in 1963 was shipped with stamped 15-inch diameter steel wheels. They were 5-1/2 inches wide and had a 5-lug pattern. The wheels were painted to match the color of the car unless the customer ordered the four-ply nylon tires. In those cases they were painted black. A few variations were allowed. Customers could special order black wheels on any color car, silver wheels were available on cars painted Sebring Silver and Silver Blue, red wheels could be ordered on cars painted Riverside Red, and blue wheels were available on cars painted Daytona Blue.

The hubcaps on the 1963 had a fake "spinner" bolt in the center. Six spokes radiated from the center of the cap to the hubcap's thin outer ring. Under the spokes was a solid "pie pan"-like disc that had a matte finish on early 1963s and a brighter finish on later 1963s. There was an optional wheel listed in 1963—the P48 Cast Aluminum Knock-Off Wheel. The lightweight, stylish wheels were a big deal in 1963 and their price tag of $322 reflected it. Aluminum wheels were pretty much an unknown quality and Chevrolet never lost a chance to promote their greatness. While the wheels were lightweight and looked great, they did have two problems. They did not hold air and the tire's beads tended to not seat properly. The general consensus in the Corvette community is that no 1963s left the factory with the P48 option. The people who ordered them were told that Chevrolet was having supply problems and to enjoy their new steel wheels.

The standard tire for 1963 was a rayon blackwall. All tires, whether base or optional, were a 6.79 x 15 size. The Corvette factory used Goodyear, Firestone, B.F. Goodrich, General, and U.S. Royal as tire suppliers for both the standard and optional tires. The option list carried two tires in 1963—the P91 Blackwall and the P92 Whitewall. The nylon blackwall tires cost an additional $16 (set) and were put on only 412 Corvettes. A set of the P92 rayon whitewalls was $32 and came on 19,383 (about 90 percent) of the Corvettes produced in 1963.

THE Z06 OPTION

There was one real option available for a dramatic improvement to the 1963 Corvette's suspension and brakes—the Z06 option. This code was offered only in 1963 and would not be available again until 2001. The Z06 was the factory method for putting the Corvette in "factory" race trim. The option was produced in five production runs and totaled 199 cars. The first of the Z06s were supplied to racers, but the public could order the option for street use. The standard springs were pulled and replaced by stiffer coil springs in the front, and the nine-leaf rear spring was replaced with a seven-leaf spring. The suspension also got special performance shocks on both front and rear.

Engineers also took a stab at improving the Corvette's less than spectacular braking ability. While the car still had drum brakes on all four corners, it was a very different setup from the standard braking system. The system would be a dual circuit (separate lines for front and rear brakes beginning at the master cylinder), which provided more pressure to the wheel cylinders. The system also

featured large metallic linings and a different self-adjuster system. Brake cooling was improved by using finned drums, vented backing plates, and small cooling fans in the drums.

When the Z06 package was introduced it had to be accompanied with the purchase of the 36-gallon fuel tank, aluminum knock-off wheels, and the 360-hp L84 fuel-injected engine. In early 1963 the mandate to purchase the wheels and the big gas tank were dropped. Still, buying a Z06 was an expensive proposition. The cost of the many unique parts (especially in the braking system) was passed along to the customer, meaning that the Z06 option alone listed for $1,818.45. When this was added to the $430.40 required to buy the fuel-injected motor, the $202.30 to buy the 36-gallon tank, and the $322.80 for the knock-off wheels, the list price of a Z06 option could be as high as $2,770.

1963 SALES REVIEW

As the Sting Ray prepared to enter its second year of production it did so with momentum. When the 1963 Corvette sales figures were totaled, the results were quite favorable when compared to the car's historic sales. Whenever a completely new automotive platform is introduced there are no assurances of success. The designers

and engineers know that the response from the buying public can range from profitable approval to disastrous disapproval. In the late 1950s and early 1960s, Corvette sales had begun to climb, peaking at 14,531 in 1962. While the Corvette team was hoping to increase sales with their radically changed body and suspension, there was certainly a chance of disappointing the thousands who had purchased the previous, but very different, Corvette.

The factory target for Corvette production was 30,000 cars. Sales for 1963 fell short of that mark, but they made it over the 20,000-unit mark for the first time. This was quite an accomplishment considering that from 1953 to 1962 Chevrolet produced a total of 69,015 Corvettes for an average yearly sales number of just over 6,900 units per year. The final tally for 1963 was 21,513 Corvettes split between 10,594 coupes and 10,919 convertibles. In total units, this was a 48-percent increase in sales from 1962 and a 97-percent increase compared to 1961. In terms of revenue for Chevrolet, the 21,513 units represented 89 million dollars based on standard pricing. For 1962 this number was 58 million dollars. Another 14 million dollars or so was achieved via the option list for a total of almost 103 million dollars.

The standard wheel offered in 1963 was a 15 x 5 steel wheel with a full-sized wheel cover. The wheel covers changed every year during C2 production.

The C2 was never consistently raced with full factory support. This was not the fault of the car, the designers, or the competition. It was more the fault of the General Motors executives. In the late 1950s a "June Cleaver" attitude toward speed prevailed with much of the public. The cars produced in Detroit were becoming bigger and faster than in previous decades and accidents were becoming more and more catastrophic, especially when high speed was involved. The large automakers were frightened that a factory supported racing effort would hurt sales with the safety conscious public. So, in the late 1950s the "Big Three" signed a pact agreeing to stay out of racing. Some of the public and some of the executives praised the decision, but others on both sides of the equation did not. While they had to operate in a very low-key manner, some at the factory continued to play around with the high performance stuff, most often under the banner of research. At the same time there was another series of events that would eventually have an impact on the Corvette racing possibilities.

These were the events surrounding an unsuccessful Texas chicken farmer with a love for overalls named Carroll Shelby. When his chicken raising days were over, Shelby became one of the most revered American road racers. His driving career peaked in 1959 when he and Roy Salvadori drove an Aston Martin to a victory in the 24 Hours of Le Mans race. He previously won the U.S. SCCA Sports Car championship driving a Ferrari in 1956. While he was a great car driver, Shelby also wanted to be a car builder. In his road racing days he was able to see how Ferrari, Maserati, and others built low volume sports cars—for a profit.

After retiring from driving in 1960, Shelby began his pursuit of building his own car. After a couple of unsuccessful attempts he went to Chevrolet in an effort at producing a racing sports car. His idea was to take a Corvette, cut a lot of weight out of it, leave the big powerful V-8, and go racing. He brought up the idea to a Chevrolet executive and was given three Corvettes—but politics intervened. One day the executive

called Shelby and announced that everyone (including a mad Duntov) had found out what he was doing. He said that the deal was over—complete lack of factory support. So the project died and Shelby went elsewhere. But this incident was not the end of Shelby's impact on the Corvette's racing future. Duntov had his own ideas of racing the Corvette and they did not include Carroll Shelby.

As the C2 began its production life in 1963, the first racing oriented option appeared in the form of the Z06 option described in Chapter 1. This option, combined with the L84 engine, the 36-gallon fuel tank, and the lightweight wheels also upgraded the brakes and suspension. A good bit of effort was spent on the brakes, the C2's glaring weakness, but they were still not up to racing form. During this period most of the European cars were lighter, with good suspensions and brakes. The Corvette's weight and inability to slow quickly never allowed its biggest asset—horsepower—to become a factor. Amateur racers had very limited success with the Z06s for these two reasons—weight and brakes. The Z06 had more motor than many of the European competition but was much heavier. Even when improved over the stock system, the drum brakes were not up to par. When combined with the car's weight, the Z06 lost a lot of ground entering the turns. This was bad news. The good news was that the Corvette's chassis and suspension was proving to be very competitive and the horsepower of the 327 was more than adequate. Were it not for the ban on racing, the Corvette team (led by Duntov) knew they could build a car that would not only compete but also actually win. In large part it was thanks to Carroll Shelby and to Ford that Duntov would get the opportunity to build his racecar.

After the Corvette fiasco, Shelby began working on another car. He took an AC body and chassis, which was manufactured in England, and added a V-8—a Ford V-8. The project started with smaller V-8s, but displacement would rise to 260 and then to 289 cubic inches. In 1962 Ford worked around the racing ban and began to back Carroll Shelby and his new Cobra racer. The Cobra was fast and competitive. It was lightweight, had disc brakes, and plenty of V-8 power. The suspension was nothing to write home about, but with a good driver the little car could be steered with the throttle. Right off the bat the Cobra was a force to be reckoned with. The Corvette won

Grand Sport 001 was the first Grand Sport built. It began life as a coupe, but in preparation for the '64 Daytona 24-hour race was decapitated to decrease drag. After GM's final racing ban in July of 1963, the car sat idle until it was sold in 1965 to Roger Penske. Penske installed a prototype L-88 engine into the car for the 1966 Sebring 12-hour race. In the early stages of the race it ran sixth overall until an off-course excursion broke an oil cooler and put it out of the race. It was clocked at over 190 miles per hour. (Bill Erdman Photography)

Like Grand Sport 001, Grand Sport 002 had the roof cut off in preparation for the 1964 13-hour race at Daytona. It was a race that neither car would be in as the GM brass banned them from the track. (Bill Erdman Photography)

in their first meeting, but only because the Cobra lost an axle after building a huge lead and had to retire from the race. After that the Cobra unleashed some pretty embarrassing whoopins on the Corvette. The races were never even close.

There are few certain rules in the universe—one is that if you want to get Chevrolet to do something, get Ford to do it first. With the Cobra project in full swing, there was no telling where it could go. Ford could conceivably have a huge impact on Corvette sales with a faster car on the track. A win on Sunday means sales on Monday. This fact combined with the blind hatred of running second to Ford in any form or fashion led Chevrolet management to an important decision. Duntov was given permission to build a Corvette that would beat the Cobra—the Grand Sport.

To race in their endurance GT classes, the FIA required the manufacturer to produce at least 100 cars per year of the model being raced. The initial plan for the Grand Sport was to build 125. The Grand Sport would rely on some of the street Corvette's parts, but it would be engineered quite differently. The biggest difference was the chassis. The steel birdcage used around the interior of the stock Corvette was replaced with a lightweight tubular version in an effort to shed weight. The tubular chassis supported a fiberglass body that looked much like the stock body; however, it was made with body panels that were much thinner than stock. The heavy steel wheels used on the street car were replaced with lightweight magnesium wheels. Throughout the car the engineers took weight where they could loose a couple of pounds here and a couple of pounds there.

As a result of all of this dieting the car was significantly lighter when put on the scales. The stock 1963 weighed in at around 3,100 pounds, while the Grand Sport weighed in at a little less than 2,000 pounds. With the weight problem solved the braking problem was attacked. The four-wheel drum brakes were thrown away and replaced with a set of large heavy-duty disc brakes on both front and rear. Engineers had planned on dropping a new 377 cubic inch engine in the Grand Sport, but the chassis and body were completed before the engine so a modified L-84 327 was used. So began the first production run of Grand Sports, which consisted of five cars. When complete they would head to the track—or not. When the cars were tested in late 1962 word got back to top executives and once again a racing ban was announced. The cars were then loaned to private racers and ran primarily on the SCCA series. One Grand Sport, Number 004, won the SCCA Nationals at Watkins Glen. Since the cars looked much like the stock Corvette, the top brass at GM were kept in the dark. The cars that raced in SCCA events were returned to Chevrolet in late 1963.

The time on the SCCA circuit helped the factory engineers. The car was modified to help solve some problems that were discovered. Vents were added to help brake cooling, wider tires were added and the hood received some radical vents as well. This was done in an effort to relieve lifting pressures on the long front of the car, helping it stay on the track. With their gained knowledge, the clandestine racing effort was continued despite the ban (now bans) on racing. The group left the country and went racing in the Bahamas. Three Grand Sports made the trip under the guise of being raced by a private racing team. Coincidentally, some Chevy engineers took their vacation in Nassau at the same time. It was here that an epic Grand Sport versus Cobra battle was to take place. The venue was the Bahamas Speed Week that featured a number of separate races. In the Governor's race, Roger Penske drove a Grand Sport to a win in the prototype class and a third place overall finish. The two other Grand Sports finished second and third in their class and an overall finish of fourth and sixth.

The next day a 252-mile race known as the Nassau Trophy race was held. Two Grand Sports ran in the race, taking first and third in the prototype class and a fourth and eighth overall. When the dust had settled it was the Grand Sport that was still standing. The Corvette soundly beat the Cobra in both races. The cars were shipped home and the excited engineers began preparing two cars for the 1964 Daytona endurance race. To cut drag, two of the cars had the roofs cut off during the preparations. But the Grand Sport's success had spelled its doom. The good run at Nassau had generated a fair amount of media coverage that was ultimately seen by the top GM brass. Yet another edict was issued demanding racing involvement to cease and for the five Grand Sports to be destroyed. The engineers who had worked so hard on the cars were unable to do so. The coupes were sold to private racers; the roadsters hidden in a warehouse and later sold to Roger Penske. So the brief racing life of the Grand Sport program ended. The program died, but all five cars survived and today are the most desirable and valuable Corvettes in existence.

Grand Sport 003 kept its top throughout its life. This was the car that Roger Penske drove to a win in the prototype class and a third overall finish in the 1963 Governor's Cup race in Nassau. (Bill Erdman Photography)

Grand Sport 004 was just behind Grand Sport 003 in the Bahamas. This car finished second in the prototype class and fourth overall, well ahead of any of the dreaded Cobras. (Bill Erdman Photography)

Printed to 1/24 scale

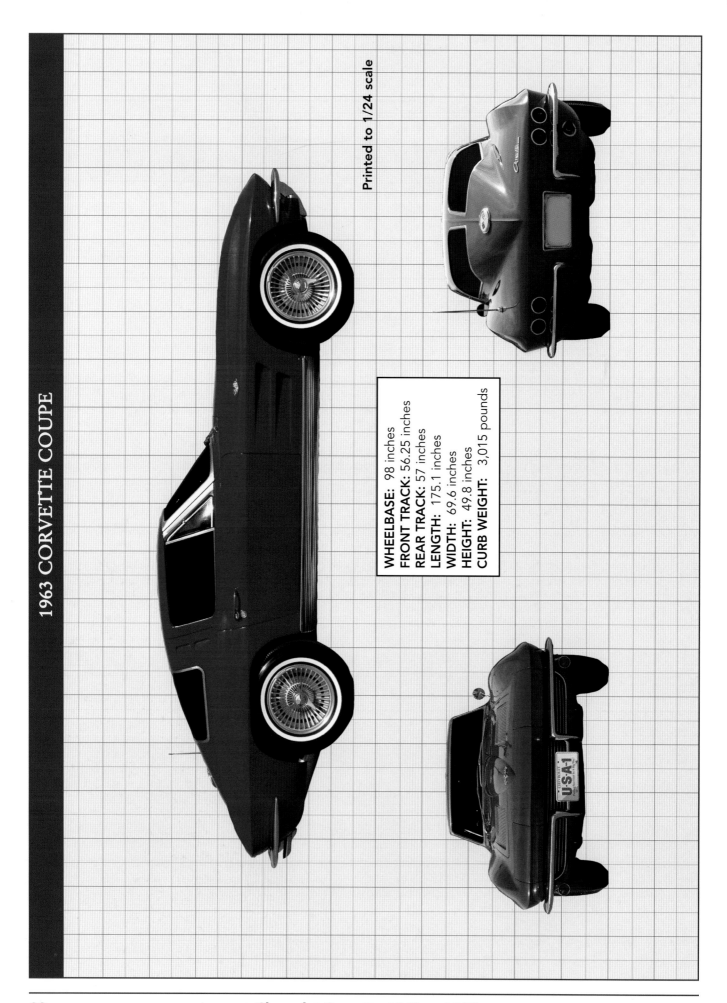

WHEELBASE: 98 inches
FRONT TRACK: 56.25 inches
REAR TRACK: 57 inches
LENGTH: 175.1 inches
WIDTH: 69.6 inches
HEIGHT: 49.8 inches
CURB WEIGHT: 3,015 pounds

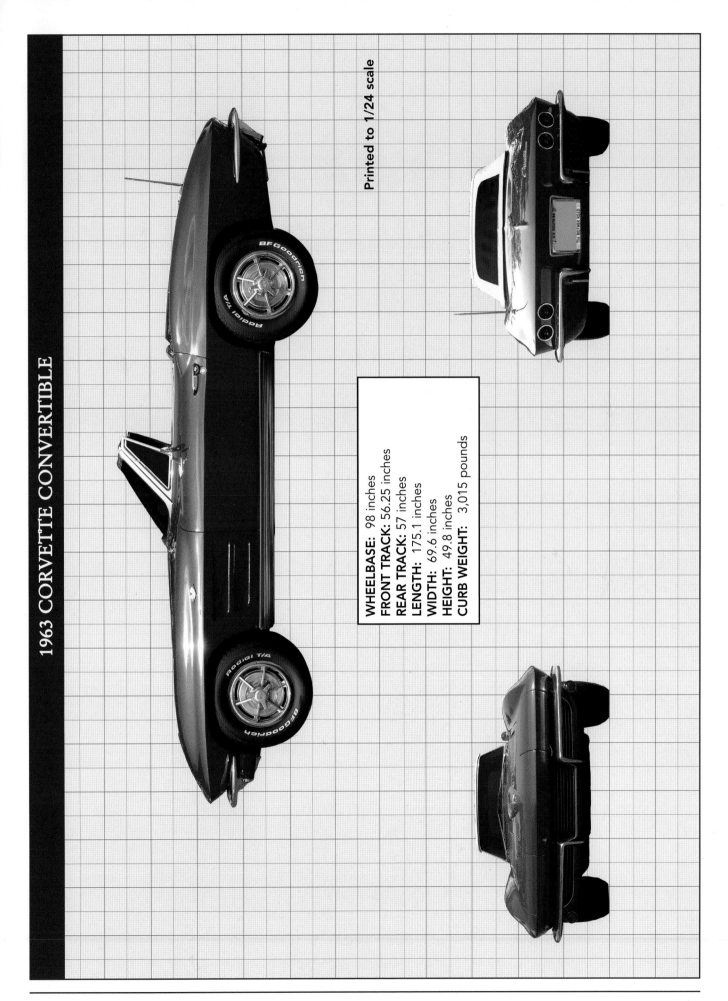

1963 CORVETTE CONVERTIBLE

Printed to 1/24 scale

WHEELBASE: 98 inches
FRONT TRACK: 56.25 inches
REAR TRACK: 57 inches
LENGTH: 175.1 inches
WIDTH: 69.6 inches
HEIGHT: 49.8 inches
CURB WEIGHT: 3,015 pounds

CHAPTER

2

1964 CORVETTE

For the 1964 sales season the price of the convertible stayed the same at $4,037 while the price of the coupe actually dropped $5 to $4,252. As 1963 was an introductory year for the new Sting Ray, there were few major changes to the chassis and body for 1964. Most of the changes were made in an attempt to eliminate minor annoyances in the 1963 model. The new body had been a hit in 1963 and Chevrolet knew it had a winner as sales numbers showed customers had accepted the car. The only ones who were a bit unhappy were the high-speed junkies. In developing the Sting Ray, Chevrolet made use of wind tunnels in an attempt to improve the aerodynamics of the car's body. It succeeded—kind of. Modern racers, open wheel and stock car, are very familiar with the swings and roundabouts of aerodynamics that are based on drag and downforce. The sleeker an object is, the more efficiently it cuts through the air. Just as a speedboat has less drag than a barge, a 1963 Corvette (pointy and sloped) cuts through the air better than a boxy car. However, when going fast, especially

when turning, downforce becomes very important. Modern racecars use spoilers and the car's body profile to get passing air to push the car down, improving handling. The Corvette engineers designed a car with pretty low drag (for the times). The problem was that little attention was paid to downforce. The C2's body actually had a profile much like an airplane wing, which produces lift. As the air passes over the top of the car it has to travel further and thus moves faster. This creates negative pressure in relation to the bottom surface, creates lift. To add to the problem, the area under the bumper was angled back. This very stylish front end worked to cram lots of air under the car as speed increased. As a result, the faster you go in a C2, the more the car wants to lift. This really wasn't a problem driving around town at reasonable highway speed or during a quick burst of acceleration, but people who bought optional powerful engines were in some danger of lift. With the L86 fuel-injected engine and a 3.70:1 rear gear, the car was capable of about 150 miles per hour. When doing so it

felt like the car was touching the ground about every 100 feet. It was decades before the Corvette became a comfortable high-speed machine. C2 owners were stuck between comfortable acceleration and frightening speed.

CHASSIS & BODY

A couple of small changes were made to the frame of the 1964 model. A new parking brake with two brackets was welded to the frame with a hole for the parking brake cable in the transmission crossmember. The body mounting points were also improved in an attempt to eliminate a bit of interior noise, which was most noticeable in the coupes. The body would undergo a major change in 1963. Bill Mitchell had insisted on the split rear window for the 1963 coupe's body. His reasons were almost purely based on styling. It might be argued that the post dividing the window added strength, which helped safety, but the safety argument could be thrown in the other direction. The rear post was a major hindrance to rear vision. Mitchell won the battle for the

With 1963 providing Chevrolet with record Corvette sales, the Corvette team was able to look to the future. At the same time they began making modifications to the car to work out a few bugs. Nineteen sixty-four would be the last year for the double alcoves located just behind the front tires. These accents are considered by many to be the most artistic and graceful of any C2, yet they only lasted two years.

Buyers flocked to the dealerships in 1963 to pay the relatively high price required to own a Corvette. In 1964, sales rose slightly to 22,229 units sold. The 50/50 split between coupes and convertibles began to skew in 1964, with 13,925 convertibles being sold against only 8,304 coupes.

For 1964 buyers could choose between seven exterior colors. This coupe is painted Daytona Blue, which was one of the car's darker and more stately colors. It often takes two looks to make sure that a Daytona Blue car is not black.

Right: When the 1964s hit the street it was obvious that there were some significant changes. The biggest change was the elimination of the post that bisected the rear window. Duntov and Shinoda won the "lack of rear visibility argument" and the post was removed, forever securing the 1963's fame.

Below: The new window was a one-piece unit surrounded with bright metal trim. While rear-view vision in any C2 coupe was not excellent, the '64 offered more visibility behind than a '63. Although the center post was removed from the rear, the raised "spine" still graced the roof and the deck lid of both coupe and convertible.

Convertible tops were available in black, white, or beige just as in 1963. While the convertible could not have the spine feature on the roof, the spine did run all the way from the rear of the cockpit to the rear of the car.

1963 production year, but Duntov won the war for 1964. The rear window became a one-piece unit and though the rear window sloped, it did not offer any greater vision than the split window. The change would ensure one other thing—the fame of the "Split Window." Its divided rear window would always rapidly identify the 1963 and when the classic Corvette craze gained steam in the 1980s, its uniqueness would translate into high value. Some of the most desirable, and thus expensive, classic C2s are the 1963 Split Window Coupes.

The same hood used in 1963 was carried over to 1964, but styled differently. The hood intakes were not functional in 1963 and with the attachment problems associated with the grille inserts they were nothing but a liability. The inserts were discontinued in 1964, but the same hood was used and it kept the recessed areas on each side.

At the front of each recessed section was a small drainage hole to keep water from pooling. Another minor change to the body was the evolution of the slots on the rear pillar behind the side windows.

The 1963 had two scalloped vents per side. They were purely for styling in 1963, but in 1964 they were made functional and the vents became a pick-up point for fresh air to better ventilate the interior of the coupe. It still had two vents per side, but they did not have slotted covers. The air picked up through the vents was blown with a fan located in front of the left rear wheel.

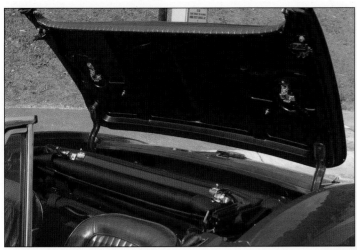

The C2 featured one of the finest convertible systems ever. By releasing four roof clamps and opening the storage door, the loose roof was folded rearward and stored under the rear deck. When the door was closed the roof was completely hidden, giving the C2 a true roofless roadster look.

Pegs on the bottom rear of the top were inserted in these fittings that were located on each side of the storage compartment's door. The small lever released the rear of the top.

On the underside of the door this spring-loaded latch held the rear of the top secure.

This latch held the convertible's hideaway door secure. A center lever at the front of the door released it.

The 1964 hood was the same as the 1963 with one exception—the hood grilles were gone. Since they had never worked as functional intakes (the reason for their existence) and they had a habit of detaching themselves in flight, they were scrapped completely. The depressions into which the grilles were mounted remained and were painted with the rest of the hood. The result gave the hood a much cleaner, slicker look. A small hole was drilled in the front corner of each hood depression to keep water from pooling when the car was parked in the rain.

The small twin coves on the pillar behind the window disappeared after just one year and were replaced with two functional vents.

The exhaust bezel on the '64 was a bit larger than on the '63. The exhaust still exited via chrome tips on each exhaust pipe.

The rocker panels were also changed from the 1963 and now featured three recessed black stripes. Rocker panels would be one of the few items that changed frequently on the C2.

The change was made with good intentions, but the system operated poorly at best.

Both coupe and convertible shared a couple of other mild changes. The rear exhaust bezels that surrounded the exhaust tips were made a bit larger in 1964. Another cosmetic change for 1964 was a new rocker cover.

The eight-rib design used in 1963 was replaced with a three-rib design for 1964. The top of the ribs had a chrome finish while the depressions were painted flat black. The doors changed slightly during the 1964 production year.

The 1963 and early 1964 models had a raised element on the door at the mounting point for the door handle. This was eliminated about midyear in the 1964 production run. The small door that accessed the gas filler also changed.

The door mechanism was the same, but in 1964 the emblem was changed to crossed flags on a silver center circle surrounded by a silver-white outer circle featuring concentric ridges. A chrome ring surrounded the entire door lid.

BODY OPTIONS

Options that affected the body also stayed much the same in 1964. The A01 and A02 Soft Ray Tinting options were still available and became much more popular. While the two combined were only put on about 1,000 1963 Corvettes, over 12,000 1964s had one of the two options. The C07 hardtop for the convertible also became more popular, with 7,023 being shipped. The biggest gainer of the body-related options was the T86 Back-up Lights.

The raised area where the door handle was mounted was used on all 1963 and early 1964 models.

The gas filler door began its habit of yearly change in 1964. The new lid still featured the crossed flags, but was now surrounded by a field of concentric rings with a thick chrome border.

The car on the left has the standard taillight arrangement. The car on the right has an optional light arrangement. When the T86 Back-up Lights were purchased the inner taillight bezels contained a clear lens in place of the red lens. While the back-up lights were helpful in certain circumstances, their existence meant the brake light display was cut in half.

This $10 option was added to only 318 1963s, but was added to 11,085 1964s. The back-up light option was still installed by replacing the inner taillight housing with a clear lens and the back-up light.

INTERIOR

The structural part of the dash, the carpet, and the door panels stayed the same as those in the 1963 model. Within the dash there were a few small changes. In front of the driver the gauges differed a bit from the 1963.

The letters and numbers on the gauges were the same, but the concave center cone was now painted black and had ridges in a circular pattern. The only 1963 gauge to keep a plastic lens was the odometer. All of the other gauges were now covered with concave-shaped glass lenses.

A few changes also took place in front of the passenger. The 1963 glove box door was made of molded plastic, but in 1964 a new glove box door appeared. It had an insert with a brushed aluminum surface surrounded by a black painted surface with a crinkled finish. Both were trimmed with a thin chrome line. The glove box latch/lock was still at the top with the emblem mounted in the lower right corner that featured "Corvette" in scripted letters and "Sting Ray" in block letters.

Behind the seats the only interior change was the addition of a chrome metal bezel for the finger pull hole on

Few changes were made to the interior of the Corvette between 1963 and 1964, and really there was no need. The press and the public had enthusiastically received the style and functionality of the cockpit.

The interior colors available changed for 1964. Black, Saddle, and red were carried over from the previous year and were joined by silver and white.

While comfortable for a sports car, the driver's area of the C2 was all business. Some early 1964s had a few features of the 1963 before changes were made midyear. The door panel is one example. Early '64s had the "dummy" twin to the door lock at the top rear of the door panel. It was eliminated later in the '64 production run.

the compartment door. The most obvious change to the interior of the 1964 was the seats. The tapering present on the seat backs of the 1963 was scrapped and replaced with bulkier seats backs for 1964.

The new backs were square with no taper. The seats had vertical stitching with seams about an inch apart surrounded by an open border.

1964 held more choices than ever when deciding on the interior color scheme for a Corvette. The base four color choices for the Corvette's interior were black, red, blue, and Saddle. The Fawn color available in 1963 was discontinued. For no additional cost the standard interior could be purchased with vinyl seats and any of these colors. These four interiors were solid in color with door panels, seats, and carpet all sporting the same color.

For the 1964 sales year Chevrolet also offered a new and stylish choice—the two-tone interior, which came in six color packages. They included silver and black, silver and blue, white and black, white and blue, white and red, and white and Saddle. This gave the buyer an unprecedented 10 standard interior color schemes at no extra cost.

The gauge arrangement stayed the same for 1964, but the gauge lenses changed. The plastic lenses used in 1963 were discontinued and replaced with glass lenses. Only the small odometer lens remained plastic.

The instrument panel on the '64 was the same as the '63 with the exception of the gauge faces. The silver centers in the '63 gauges were replaced with black centers with concentric ridges that were much less likely to create a glare.

Of course cars produced with a Powerglide automatic transmission were clutchless. The small brake pedal used on manual transmission cars was replaced with a wider brake pedal on cars equipped with automatics.

Lap belts were still the standard in 1964 with the adjuster on the outboard buckle half. Shoulder belts were never standard equipment on the C2, but they appeared as an option in 1966.

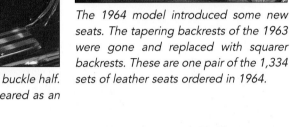

The 1964 model introduced some new seats. The tapering backrests of the 1963 were gone and replaced with squarer backrests. These are one pair of the 1,334 sets of leather seats ordered in 1964.

On a car with the two-tone interior, the seatbelt color matches the carpet and not the seats.

INTERIOR OPTIONS

If buyers chose to furnish their 1964 Corvette interior with all of the available interior options it would set them back about $750. The total number of interior options available was down to five in 1964, and one of these was not really an option but a deletion. Under the C48 code an "ultra performance" buyer could eliminate the heater and defroster systems and receive a $100 credit. This left only four optional interior items. Leather seats were again available for a mere $80, yet only 1,334 1964 Corvettes had them. The leather seats were available in both solid and two-tone interiors.

The $59 A31 power window option was still around, but was actually less popular with buyers in 1964, with only 3,706 being made. In 1964 air conditioning became a more common option on Corvettes. This option was included with 1,988 1964 Corvettes as opposed to 278 in 1963. The system

Most cars were shipped with vinyl seats like these. A small, low armrest was located between the seats.

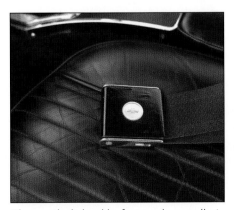

The seatbelt buckle featured a small circular center detail with a Chevy bowtie.

The face of the glove box was changed from plastic to brushed aluminum in 1964. It still featured its black border and Corvette Sting Ray emblem in the lower left corner.

The car's ID tags were attached to a bulkhead under the passenger's side dash. These tags carry the car's VIN as well as the paint and interior codes.

The plate surrounding the shifter was changed for 1964. The all-metal look of the '63 was replaced with a plate that was partially painted to match the car's interior color. The arrangement of the shifter, ashtray, and shift pattern diagram stayed the same.

The shifters on both manual and automatic equipped cars were very similar in appearance. Both featured a chrome shift lever with a black shift knob. The automatic did not have the "T"-shaped reverse lockout lever or a different shift pattern indicator plate.

The carpet used in '64 was a carryover from '63 and was still made with flat pieces of custom-cut nylon carpet sewed where necessary. It disappeared in 1965 and was replaced by molded carpet. The molded carpet was installed on a few cars late in 1964.

(under code C60) remained a pricey $421. By far the most popular interior option item was the U69 AM-FM Radio, which was installed on 20,934 of the 22,229 1964 Corvettes produced. FM technology was still pretty new in 1964 and as a result was very expensive. The U69's price of $176 is now somewhat staggering. A buyer could equip his 1964 Corvette with power steering, power brakes, and a performance suspension for less than the cost of the U69 radio. Another option—the N32 wood-grained wheel—was offered on the option list, but according to records none were actually bolted onto a 1964 Corvette. The only interior option item that was available in 1963 and dropped in 1964 was the U85 signal-seeking AM radio.

ENGINE & DRIVETRAIN

Under the hood the 1964 Corvette was also much like the 1963. While it had some minor changes and minor horsepower improvements, the codes of the engines offered remained the same. It would be another year before Chevrolet began to really play with what was available under the hood.

The base engine for the 1964 was still the 327 rated at 250 horsepower at 4,400 rpm, and 350 ft-lbs of torque at 2,800 rpm. It had 10.50:1 compression, hydraulic lifters, and a Carter four-barrel carburetor. It was not significantly

The door panels changed slightly during the 1964 production year. The panels were essentially the same as those used in 1963 until the second knob that complemented the door lock was removed. The positions of the window cranks and door latch stayed the same.

Solid-metal sill plates protected the bottom of the doorway on the '64. The molding had a raised jam to the inside and its surface was textured with two sections of small ridges.

The mainstay of the C2 engine lineup remained the 327. The base motor was rated by the factory at 250 horsepower with 10.50:1 compression and a Carter four-barrel carburetor.

The base engine featured an air cleaner housing with twin forward-facing snorkel air intakes. The housing was black with a chrome top.

Forward of all engines was a tight-fitting shroud to allow the fan to efficiently pull air. Every Corvette had a performance engine crammed into a small space with a pretty small air intake area out front. For designers, overheating was always a concern.

different from the 1963 base engine. The first optional engine was still the L75. It was not changed much from 1963, producing 300 horsepower at 5,000 rpm and 360 ft-lbs of torque at 3,200 rpm. It, too, had hydraulic lifters and a Carter four-barrel carburetor. About the only visible difference in the 1964 version was the relocation of the crankcase vent to the rear of the air cleaner's base plate on non-air conditioned cars.

The powerful L76 was also carried over from 1963, but underwent some significant internal changes. The valvetrain and fuel delivery system were modified. A higher-pressure fuel pump was added to supply gas to the new low-profile Holley carburetor, which replaced the Carter used on the 1963 L76. A new intake manifold was also introduced. With these changes the power ratings of the L76 were changed. The engine was now rated at 365 horsepower at 6,200 rpm and 350 ft-lbs of torque at 4,000 rpm. The engine kept its 11.25:1 compression ratio and mechanical lifters. The top of the line in Corvette motors remained the L84. It, too, went through some internal changes between the 1963 and 1964 production schedule. Like the L76, the changes to the L84 were a matter of internal massaging. With some work on the valvetrain, some porting changes, and a revised camshaft, horsepower was bumped up from 360 at 6,000 rpm to 375 at 6,200 rpm. Torque for the 1964 L84 was rated at 350 ft-lbs at 4,800 rpm.

The distributor, wires, and plugs retained their intricate armor in order to help eliminate electrical interference and to protect the ignition system.

The optional L76 produced 365 horsepower and was the most powerful carbureted Corvette engine in 1964. The L76 had 11.25:1 compression and was fed with a Holley carburetor. About a third of the '64s produced came with this engine. When the buyer upgraded to the L76 he received an engine with an entirely different appearance. The base engine's air cleaner housing was replaced with an open element performance unit that sported a chrome lid. The valve covers were replaced with great looking finned aluminum covers that Corvette scripted along the top.

Road Exhaust System and the N03 36-Gallon Fuel Tank options were carried over from 1963. The $37 N11 was added to 1,953 1964s, while the $202 N03 was installed in only 552 Corvettes, all coupes.

DRIVELINE

The powertrain remained the same as the 1963. The M20 four-speed and the M35 Powerglide were still the only optional transmissions and again were installed on 97 percent of the Corvettes produced. As sales increased in 1964, so did the shipment of M20s, but the sales of Powerglides dropped. Corvettes that left the factory with an M20 equaled 19,043, yet only 2,480 were shipped with a Powerglide. The Corvette buyer's love of the G81 Positraction option also continued. In 1964, 18,279 of the 22,229 Corvettes produced had Positraction. The gear choices for 1964 included the 3.08:1, 3.36:1, 3.55:1, 3.70:1, 4.11:1, and the 4.56:1.

SUSPENSION, STEERING & BRAKES

The stock suspension and steering system stayed pretty much the same as the 1963, but again with subtle differences. The parts and design remained the same, but the geometry was tuned a bit to improve ride comfort. The biggest change in the area of the suspension was the appearance of RPO

The L83 was still fueled with the Rochester mechanical fuel injector and relied on mechanical lifters.

ENGINE OPTIONS

A new option for 1964 was the K66 Transistor Ignition System. This 475 option replaced the standard ignition system with one of General Motors' first electronically controlled ignitions. The system was state-of-the-art technology for the mid '60s and was a glimpse of things to come. The K66 was only installed in 552 1964 Corvettes, representing less than 3 percent of total production. The N11 Off-

Cars equipped with the Powerglide transmission had an additional dipstick just forward of the firewall to register the transmission's fluid level.

All 1964 Corvettes featured a radiator expansion tank that was both businesslike and elegant. The filling instructions were imprinted on the tank's side.

The buyer's engine choice had a small impact on the instrument panels—different engines had different redlines. The base engine's tach had a 5,500-rpm redline, while the powerful L76 had a tach that redlined at 6,500 rpm.

The suspension did not have any significant changes between 1963 and 1964. The front suspension still featured large drum brakes.

F40 on the option list. It was a code (later changed to F41) that remained around for a while and became synonymous with Chevrolet performance suspensions. The Z06 code that was used in 1963 for a performance suspension was discontinued. Taking its place, the F40 was a major performance upgrade to the suspension. Like the Z06, the F40 added stiffer coil springs to the front and replaced the 9-leaf rear spring with a stiffer 7-leaf unit. The F40 also replaced the .75-inch front sway bar with a beefier .375-inch bar. Unlike the Z06, the F40 did not change the car's brake system.

The power steering system was also still available and 3,126 buyers, about 14 percent, shelled out the $75 required to purchase the system, still coded as N40. The brakes of the 1964 were also a carryover from 1963, but

The rear drums were a bit smaller than the front drums. The shock absorber was strung between the frame rail and the trailing arm just forward of the wheel hub. The leaf spring end was connected to the rear of the trailing arm with a long bolt cushioned with rubber bushings.

Top left, center and above: The steering shaft exited the firewall just under the brake master cylinder. The steering gear was attached to the steering shaft with a flexible joint dampened with a cushioning material that was compressed in the coupling. The aperture for checking and replacing the lubricant was cast into the lid's surface.

Below: The power steering control valve was mounted on the left side frame rail just aft of the front left tire.

Below: Power-steering-equipped cars had the pump mounted on the left side of the engine. Power steering gained a bit in popularity in 1964 with 14 percent of the cars having the $75 system.

the option list had changed. Power brakes were still offered under the J50 code for $43, but their popularity actually dropped. In 1964 only 2,270 Corvettes were produced with the option as opposed to 3,336 in 1963. The J65 Sintered Metallic Brakes option still upgraded the car with the more efficient brake system, but the price rose from $37 to $53—the 1964 version of the option was a power brake system. The J65 was added to 4,780 Corvettes in 1964. The Special Sintered Metallic Brake Package was offered under the code J56, which was not offered in 1963. The J56 was a whopping $639 and was basically the brake system that was included in the 1963 Z06 option. Unlike the base brakes, it featured larger metallic shoes and finned drums. The

system had the dual-circuit plumbing like the Z06, but the brake shoes were a bit smaller than the Z06 shoes. As a result of the high price, only 29 1964s were equipped with the J56 option, making them quite valuable. The 1964 Corvette rode on wheels that were physically the same as the standard 15 x 5-1/2-inch steel wheels used in 1963. The only difference was that all 1964 wheels were painted gloss black, whereas most 1963 wheels were painted to match the exterior color of the car. The wheel covers for 1964 were different from those used in 1963. The 1964 wheel covers still had a fake spinner nut as a centerpiece, but the surface radiating outward was now more conical with slots as the main feature instead of spokes between the center and the rim.

Some early 1964 wheel covers had a painted finish on the center, but most came with the cover completely chromed. The P48 Cast Aluminum Knock-Off Wheels were still on the option list as a factory upgrade from the relatively heavy steel wheels. In addition to being cool, the wheels eliminated unsprung weight making them a significant performance item. In 1964 the process used to manufacture the aluminum wheels had improved and Chevrolet was actually able to get some to the customers. At year's end the factory had put the $322 set of wheels on around 800 of the cars produced. The aluminum wheels were attached to the car differently from the standard steel wheels. In place of the standard five-lug nut arrangement, the knock-offs were

964's brake system utilized a single line r cylinder with a metal lid that was held ce with a swing-away clip.

The 1964's brake system was the same as the 1963's—drum brakes on front (left) and rear (right). The wheel cylinder was located at the top with the adjustor at the bottom. This was the last year that drum brakes were the base system.

There were two ways to go when it came to the Corvette's wheels. The standard car still came with a steel wheel, but the wheel cover changed from the previous year. The cover still had a "fake" spinner, but now it had nine small slits as well.

The P48 Cast Aluminum Knock-Off Wheels made it to the streets in 1964. The rims were a pricey $322 and were only added to 806 Corvettes in '64.

secured with a single large-winged nut. The factory also included a nifty lead hammer to "knock" the wings of the large nut in order to tighten or loosen. Some who bought the wheels experienced problems. The casting technology wasn't perfected and the wheels were often still a bit porous. As a result many of the wheels would slowly lose air, depending on the quality of the cast. In 1964 the standard tire was still a rayon blackwall with a size of 6.70 x 15, but they came on few cars. The optional $31 P92 6.70 x 15 Whitewall with rayon cords was by far the most common tire, coming on 19,838 cars. The only other optional tire was the $16 P91 Blackwall. This tire was the same size, but had nylon cords and was mounted on only 412 Corvettes. The Corvette factory continued to use Goodyear, Firestone, B.F. Goodrich, General, and U.S. Royal as tire suppliers.

1964 SALES REVIEW

When reviewing the 1964 sales year, the good news was that sales had not dropped. The bad news was that they did not grow much either. At year's end Chevrolet had shipped 22,229 Corvettes split between 8,304 hardtops and 13,925 convertibles. When compared to the 21,513 sold in 1963 (split between 10,594 hardtops and 10,919 convertibles), overall sales had grown by a little over 3 percent. While it was still far short of the 30,000-unit goal, the total revenue for the 1964 production run (based on list prices) was almost 92 million dollars. Option revenue added another 15 million for a total of almost 107 million dollars for Chevrolet.

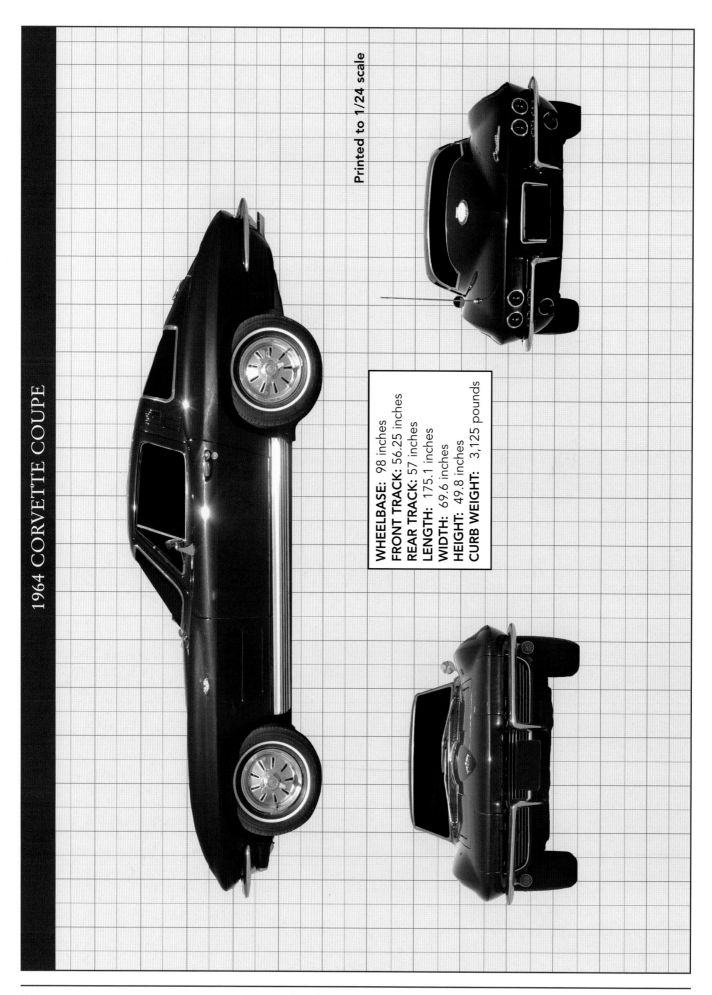

1964 CORVETTE COUPE

Printed to 1/24 scale

WHEELBASE: 98 inches
FRONT TRACK: 56.25 inches
REAR TRACK: 57 inches
LENGTH: 175.1 inches
WIDTH: 69.6 inches
HEIGHT: 49.8 inches
CURB WEIGHT: 3,125 pounds

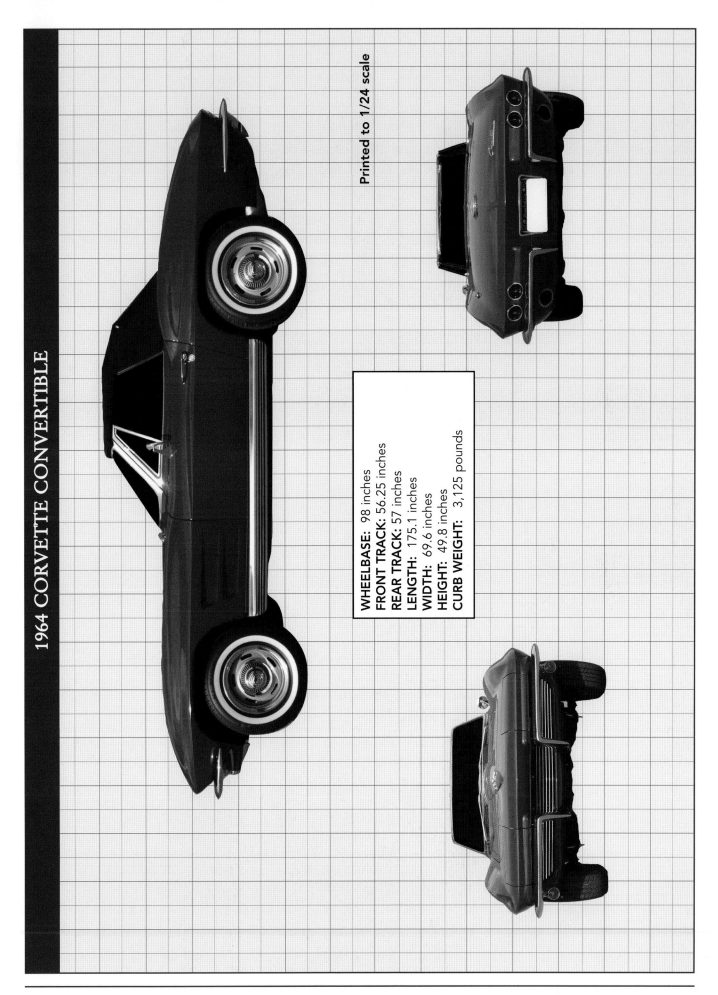

1964 CORVETTE CONVERTIBLE

Printed to 1/24 scale

WHEELBASE: 98 inches
FRONT TRACK: 56.25 inches
REAR TRACK: 57 inches
LENGTH: 175.1 inches
WIDTH: 69.6 inches
HEIGHT: 49.8 inches
CURB WEIGHT: 3,125 pounds

CHAPTER
3
1965 CORVETTE

For the 1965 sales year the Corvette's price increased $69 for both convertible and hardtop. The convertible increased from $4,252 to $4,321 and the hardtop rose from $4,037 to $4,106. With the exception of the changed rear window, visually the 1964 Corvette had been an almost direct carry-over from 1963. And while the 1965 looked much like the first two C2s, there was some very significant mechanical changes. The Corvette team went even further to supply horsepower to their customers with more powerful engines. Added to that was another—perhaps even more welcomed—change. They helped their customers slow down. It was a much-needed change. Slowing a fast running 1963 or 1964 Corvette could be an adventure. There is a reason that drum brakes have all but disappeared—they stink. That is, they stink when compared to disc brakes, which is exactly what the engineers bolted onto the 1965 Corvette. Aside from the ability to go faster and slow faster, customers saw a few other subtle differences in the 1965 offerings.

CHASSIS & BODY

Everything flows downhill, so when Corvette engineers decided to add motors and change the brakes, their actions forced changes to the chassis as well. The introduction of larger-displacement engines created a clearance problem with the cross-member due to the larger crankshaft pulley. To fix the problem the front crossmember was made with a recess, adding clearance and accommodating the bigger crank pulley. In 1965 all Corvettes, regardless of the engine, were built with the new crossmember. The sides of the frame were slightly different—a "T"-shaped slot was added to the frame rails to hang the new optional side pipes on. Like the crossmember, all 1965 Corvettes had the slots regardless of the exhaust system. As the Corvettes aged the T-slots were an area that rusted, being somewhat open to the elements.

In the rear, the frame horns were also modified. In order to fit the new braking system, engineers bent the frame horns at a different angle to cre-ate a bit of space. They also modified the bump stops that kept the trailing arms from bottoming out. The 1964 frames had welded nuts on the rear frame rails for mounting a rear sway bar in cars equipped with big-blocks or a performance suspension. The nuts were present on all cars whether they had a rear sway bar or not.

While the changes to the chassis required a bit of inspection by buyers, there were a few slight but obvious changes to the body. In the front, the chrome and black grille finish of the previous two years was dropped in favor of a blacked-out look.

While the bumpers remained chrome, the grille's horizontal elements were finished in black and surrounded by a chrome outer trim.

The hood was also different for 1965. The factory produced a new hood that eliminated the flat recessed areas, which were originally used to mount the 1963's hood grilles. The factory introduced another hood in 1965.

The big-block engine introduced to the Corvette required a bit more

The coupe retained its aggressive look in 1965; however, there were a few changes. With the addition of the big-block hood and side pipes, the 1965 was capable of an even more powerful look.

Tuxedo Black and Ermine White were the only exterior colors carried over from 1964. The new colors for '65 were Rally Red, Nassau Blue, Glen Green, Goldwood Yellow, Silver Pearl, and Milano Maroon (shown here).

Nineteen sixty-five brought major changes to the Corvette. While the car's general appearance was the same, there were significant changes to the body, brakes, and engine.

Sales of the Corvette continued to climb, taking the C2 to numbers never reached with previous models. In 1965 a total of 23,562 Corvettes were sold, split between 15,376 convertibles and 8,186 coupes.

Nassau Blue was a new color for 1965 and was the year's most popular. When production of the 1965 models ended, 6,022 of the 23,562 were painted this color. This means that more than one out of every four '65s were painted Nassau Blue.

While many elements of the 1965's body were the same as the '63 and '64, there were some differences. A new grille appeared at the front. Designers went for the "blacked out" look with the horizontal grille elements finished in black. The grille was framed with a chrome border.

The front bumpers and running lights stayed the same in 1965. These parts are interchangeable on all C2s.

Nineteen sixty-five brought a new hood to the base Corvette. The side depressions on the 1964's hood were gone. The Corvette's hood was now much flatter, but it still featured the narrow bulge from rear to front.

The new base hood was not the only new engine cover. Nineteen sixty-five brought the first "big-block hood," which was added to the car if it was equipped with the new 396-ci engine that was added to the Corvette option list in 1965. The hood allowed all to see that a special engine powered the car without having to get close enough to read the 396 badge on the fenders.

space than its small-block cousins, so the factory built a hood with a large arrowhead-shaped hump in the center. The effect was twofold. Functionally it allowed the hood to close when the bigger engine was installed. Psychologically it warned all motorists that this was not a powerful Corvette, but a ridiculously powerful Corvette.

On the side of the car the slots aft of the front wheels were changed for 1965. The stacked coves used in 1963 and 1964 were changed to three vertical slots. The rocker panels also changed for the third time in three years. The three-ribbed design of 1964 was dropped in favor of a rocker cover with only one black line on the chrome backing.

On the deck lid the door covering the fuel filler changed again. The new door featured the crossed flags but was surrounded by a black ring.

Eight exterior color choices were available in 1965. The only two carried over from 1964 were Tuxedo Black and Ermine White. The new colors included Rally Red, Nassau Blue, Silver Pearl, Glen Green, Goldwood Yellow, and Milano Maroon. It was the first time that green and yellow paint were put on a C2. No significant changes to the few options affected the body. The A01 and A02 windshield and window tinting options were carried over into 1965, as was the C07 removable hardtop for convertible buyers. The top remained popular with 7,787 of the 15,376 people that purchased convertibles in 1965 and elected to buy the $236 top.

The area behind the front wheels was changed for 1965. The twin, stacked coves that graced the first two years of C2 production were replaced with three wide vertical slots. Unlike the details on the earlier cars, these slots were true openings and did allow for some dissipation of engine heat.

The slots on the coupe's rear pillar, introduced in 1964, were carried over to the 1965 model year. While an effort was made to make the slots a functional air pickup in '64, the results were not successful and the effort was abandoned for 1965. The rear window was the same as in '64.

Convertible tops were available in black, white, and beige in 1965.

A folding steel skeleton on the inside supported the roof.

The door had a raised mounting platform for the door handle in 1963 and early 1964. It was removed during production in 1964; so all 1965s have the flush-mount door handle.

The front of the top was held in place with two clamps, one on each side of the windshield frame.

The gas cap changed once again for the 1965 sales season. The new pattern featured the crossed flags circled by a bold black ring. Other than the lid cover the mechanism was the same.

Back-up lights were only offered as an option in '63 and '64, but were made standard equipment in 1965. The lights were the same as the optional system offered previously. They provided light for backing, but also cut half of the car's brake light visibility.

INTERIOR

The interior changed slightly between 1964 and 1965. New engines and brakes took the attention and budgets of the Corvette team. Those in charge of the interior made a couple of small refinements and added one significant option.

One of the more noticeable changes was in the driver information system. In 1965 the gauges had semi-gloss faces with green silk-screened letters. Slightly modified instrument needles were introduced in 1965 that were a highly visible fluorescent orange with a small chrome base. The gauge lenses were concave with the exception of the odometer.

The Corvette's seat appearance changed again in 1965. The seat cushions had a different stitching pattern. The new seat cover was stitched so that it had two panels on the seat bottom and three on the seat back. Another change to the seat was the addition of a molded panel that covered the back of the seat.

The panel was really only visible when the seat was tilted forward. At the base, the seat rails were bolted directly to the floor of the car through a cutout in the carpet. The tab of carpet from the cutout remained and covered the rail once the seat was bolted in. Nineteen sixty-five was the first full production year to use molded carpet.

This change took place in late 1964, so it is possible for a '64 produced late in the production run to have molded carpet. The molded carpet replaced the multi-piece cut carpets of

Interior colors were expanded in 1965 to include solid interiors in black, red, blue, Saddle, Green, Maroon, and silver as well as two-tone interiors in white and red or white and blue.

As in all previous C2s, the driver of a 1965 was presented with an impressive array of gauges. The concentric ridges used in the centers of the 1964's gauges were gone after just one year. The 1965 featured flat gauge faces.

The only place for the radio speaker was between the two humps on the dash. Just ahead of the speaker grille is the windshield defroster duct.

The brushed aluminum surface that was added in 1964 was continued in 1965. Regardless of the interior color chosen, the border around the glove box door was black.

The center dash remained mostly the same from the previous year, with one minor change to its most prominent feature. The basic 1 through 12 numbers on the clock face were supplemented by a set of 13 through 24 military numbers. This greatly helped those who could buy and drive a Corvette but could not tell the difference between night and day.

The center console cover was color matched to the interior with the exception of the plate around the shifter and ashtray. The painted surface had a crinkled, textured finish.

A new seat cover accompanied the '65 off of the assembly line. The seat's shape was similar to the '64s, but the stitching changed considerably. With fewer side-to-side seams the seat bottom and backrest were "cut up" into fewer sections.

A new seat back was introduced in 1965. For the first time a plastic back was used to cover and protect the seat back. A small vent was located in the center bottom of the piece, allowing for some air circulation to allow ventilation in the seat structure.

the previous years. This made installation easier for the factory and gave the interior a more uniform look.

In 1964 the base interior colors were trimmed to four. In 1965 the number rose to eight. Both coupe and convertible could be ordered with a black, blue, green, maroon, red, Saddle, silver, or white interior. As in previous years, the interior colors were only available with certain exterior colors. The black interior was once again the only color available with all of the exterior colors. White interiors were available in cars painted any color except Silver Pearl. Red interiors were available in cars painted Tuxedo Black, Ermine White, Milano Maroon, Silver Pearl, or Rally Red. Maroon was available in cars painted Tuxedo Black, Ermine White, or Milano Maroon. Green was available in cars painted Tuxedo Black, Ermine White, or Glen Green. The Saddle interior was available in cars painted Tuxedo Black, Ermine White, Glen Green, or Milano Maroon. The new silver interior could be added to cars painted Tuxedo Black, Ermine White, or Silver Pearl.

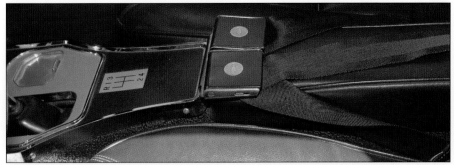

The seatbelt buckles were the same as the '64 and were color matched to the interior. When not in use they resided just forward of the padded armrest, which was too low for actual arm resting.

The outboard seatbelt section that contained the male end of the buckle sported a rubber sheath at its base.

INTERIOR OPTIONS

The option list had a new item in 1965. The C2's only adjustment to accommodate the driver's size was seat adjustment. From 1963 to 1967 this was accomplished, like most seats, with a locking rail mechanism that allowed the seat to travel forward and rearward. The mechanism to unlock the system was a lever located at the base of the seat bottom. To help create further comfort for drivers, the optional N36 Telescoping Steering Wheel was introduced. The telescoping wheel had a different center cap arrangement than the base wheel. If the car was equipped with the N36 option it had a center cap with a bowtie emblem and a locking ring with six chrome tabs. Another new item on the interior option list was the Z01 Comfort and Convenience Group. This $16 upgrade included a vanity mirror, glove box light, and backup lights. The option was added to 15,397 Corvettes in its first year. The N32 steering wheel was again offered and this time Chevrolet actually sold them. In 1965, 2,259 cars were shipped with the $48 optional teakwood rimmed steering wheel.

The option list still offered leather seats with 2,128 1965s being fit with the $80 seats. The A01 and A02 window tinting treatment options were still around, costing $16 and $10, respectively. Power windows were priced at $59 and relatively rare, coming on just 3,809 cars. Air conditioning also remained a rare commodity with only 2,423 units being sold in 1965.

The U69 AM-FM Radio remained the most popular interior option with 22,113 of the $203 units installed in 1965. The C48 heater and defroster deletion option allowed the car to be shipped without the heating and defrosting system. The option gave the buyer a $100 credit and was only selected by 39 buyers, most of whom were racers.

ENGINE & DRIVETRAIN

Since the C2 was introduced in 1963, all of its engines had been different versions of Chevrolet's 327-ci small-block V-8. For 1965, the 327 would remain the foundation for the base power plant and four optional engines, but a big brother would join it. The engine department had gotten about all of the streetable horsepower they could from 327 cubic inches, so the next logical move was to increase displacement. Chevrolet had been developing larger-displacement engines, the biggest of which was a 427-ci monster, but the 427 was not dropped into the Corvette. Not yet. General Motors' corporate policy limited engine size to 400 cubic inches in 1965, so it would be another big-block, the L78, that was added to the lineup.

Other than the introduction of the new big-block, the motor lineup was much like those of 1963 and 1964. The L84 was no longer the king of horsepower in the Corvette kingdom by 1965. The crown went to the new 396.

The door panel changed dramatically in 1965. The new door panel was a molded unit that featured an integral armrest.

By 1965 the transition from cut to molded carpet was complete, meaning all 1965 Corvettes came with molded carpet. Any edges that were visible were trimmed in vinyl.

The FM radio still represented a large investment in 1965. Even so, 22,113 1965 interiors had one of the $203 AM-FM units that was listed under code U69.

The N32 Teakwood Steering Wheel option was introduced in 1965. The wooden-rimmed wheel cost $48 and was added to fewer than 10 percent of the 1965s produced. The wheel was a much more striking piece than the plastic wood-grained wheel previously and subsequently offered. Another new option for 1965

The power antenna was activated independently of the radio. The switch was hidden on the left side of the center console.

was the N36 Telescoping Steering Wheel. This was done in an attempt to make the car comfortable for those larger or smaller than the average person. The option featured a locking ring in the center of the steering wheel. When released, it allowed the wheel to be moved forward or rearward to adjust the space between the seat and wheel. Those with short or long arms greatly benefited from the $43 option.

Leather seats were becoming a bit more popular and were added to 2,128 cars in 1965.

The 327 was still the mainstay of Corvette power in 1965. Five models of the little V-8 were available with horsepower ranging from 250 to 375.

The small-block would get a big brother in 1965. The guys at the Corvette factory were handcuffed with General Motors' policy of keeping engine displacement under 400 cubic inches, so it was the 396 that was added to the option list.

While making this change there was once again friction in the Corvette camp. We now look back nostalgically at the high compression 327s of the mid 1960s, but at the time they were really nothing all that special. The fuel-injected motor may have been unique, but a high compression, carbureted 327 was nothing unusual by 1965. Across the American automotive community more and more companies were building power. Many at Chevrolet wanted the Corvette to have the biggest and the best. Some thought that Chevrolet's 409 needed to be mated to the Corvette. Others wanted it to be another engine of more cubic inches, the 427, that was bouncing around the Chevrolet motor division. And some, led by one, wanted to stay with the lighter small-block. That one was Zora Duntov. But in the end with the pressure applied internally (and by Ford's 427 externally) Duntov was defeated. The big-block would be mated to the Corvette. The 396 had been developed at Chevrolet and was said to get its roots from the "special" Chevy engine that won the 1963 Daytona 500.

BASE ENGINE

The base engine for 1965 remained the 327 with a horsepower output of 250 at 4,400 rpm and 350 ft-lbs of torque at 2,800 rpm. There were no significant changes from the 1964 version of the engine. Once again the standard engine in a Corvette was rare. Only 2,549 (less than 10 percent) of the 23,562 Corvettes produced in 1965 had the base engine. The first step up on the performance ladder was still the L75. The engine continued to be rated at 300 horsepower at 5,000 rpm with 360 ft-lbs of torque at 3,200 rpm. Like the base engine, the L75 was not changed from the 1964 version and continued to be the choice with buyers. At the end

The cutaway air cleaner was continued and was the same as those used the previous two years.

of the year, 8,358 buyers chose the $53 L75 to provide their power. This represented over a third of total Corvette engine production. From 1963 through 1965 the L75 was one of the C2's success stories. The price of the optional engine remained at $53 over those three years and had provided 26,862 Corvette owners with powerful and dependable propulsion. The engine lineup went through some major changes in 1966 and the L75 code no longer appeared on the option list.

The 365-hp L76 was also on its way out during the 1965 sales season. The L76 had been built to fill a slot in the Corvette power lineup. For those who wanted to stay away from the relatively complex arena of mechanical fuel injection, the L76 was the most powerful engine available. In order to get an impressive 1.04-hp per cubic inch, the engine builders relied on things like a hot cam and solid lifters. The parts meant more power, but were sometimes not the best choice for a daily driver. Still, the L76 was popular, with over 5,000 being ordered in 1965. But as production ran down, so did the supply of L76s. The L76's slot in the power lineup was taken by a new big-block engine com-

ing on line. By using cubic inches Chevrolet did not have to build the engine so race-like to produce power over the 350-hp mark. The engine featured a four-barrel carburetor mounted on an aluminum manifold.

In 1965 L76s were produced with both Holley and Carter carburetors. The engine was decked out with cast-aluminum valve covers with cooling fins and a chrome air cleaner top. Transmission choices were limited to manuals and all cars with the L76 left the factory with an M20 four-speed. The L79 was a new offering in 1965. It was essentially an L76 with hydraulic lifters rated at 350 horsepower (15 horsepower less than the L76). The L79 was fueled with a Carter four-barrel on an aluminum manifold. Like the L76, the L79 had aluminum ribbed valve covers and an open-type air cleaner with a chrome top. The quickest way to spot whether the car had an L76 or L79 is the tachometer. Cars with an L76 redlined at 6,500; those with the L79 redlined at 5,500 or 6,000. The L79 was a great choice for those who wanted both increased power and drivability. In its first year 4,716 L79s were installed in Corvettes.

The birth of the big-block had its casualties. The L84 joined the L75 and L76 on the engine option death list in 1966. While the fuel-injected 327 was a powerful engine, there was much more power in cubic inches. Not only was there more power, but also it was achievable at a much lower cost with the big-blocks that were being developed. Only 771 L84s left the factory in 1965, making it the least common engine that year. There are, and always have been, proponents and critics of the mechanical fuel injector. In the end they all must agree that in the vintage

Corvette market, the old "Fuelie" cars draw a lot of attention. The L84 was unchanged from 1964 and kept its 375-hp rating. While it was still the most powerful small-block engine available in the Corvette, it was no longer Chevrolet's most powerful engine.

The newest Corvette engine, the L78 big-block, was rated at 425 horsepower at 6,000 rpm with 352 ft-lbs of torque at 4,000 rpm. It also weighed about 200 pounds more than the small-block (this was Duntov's beef). But the extra power overcame all and the 396 was a bit (not much, but a bit) faster than the more complicated and expensive fuel-injected 327. The 396 had about the same cylinder bore as the 327—4.09 inches as opposed to 4.00 inches in the 327. The big difference was the stroke, which was 3.76 inches as opposed to the 3.25-inch stroke of the 327. The result was a seemingly limitless barrage of torque when the accelerator was engaged. Rated by Chevrolet at 425 horsepower, many felt these were very conservative numbers. The engine was built with an 11.0:1 compression ratio and a 6,400-rpm redline. This made it the fastest turning Corvette engine ever. A Holley four-barrel was mounted atop an aluminum intake manifold and crowned with a chrome open-element air filter. The air cleaner lid featured a crossed-flag 396 decal forward of center and a Turbo-Jet 425-hp decal on the front edge. The exhaust system of the 396 consisted of cast performance manifolds transitioning to a 2.5-inch exhaust. As mentioned in the body section, the purchase of the 396 meant the car came with the "big-block" hood that featured a large bulge towards the rear and tapered to a point at the front of the car.

The big news in the engine department was the addition of the 396-ci L78 to the engine option list. The engine had a compression ratio of 11.0:1 and was fed by a Holley four-barrel carburetor housed under the familiar open element air cleaner.

The L78 pumped out 425 horsepower and 352 ft-lbs of torque. It cost $292 and was added to 2,157 cars during the 1965 sales campaign. It again proved to the Chevrolet executives that Corvette buyers would pay a premium for horsepower.

Another classic was introduced in 1965. The N14 Side Mount Exhaust System cost $134 and was added to only 759 cars in 1965, making them a rare find.

The exhaust pipe was shielded along the rocker and exited just in front of the rear wheel.

ENGINE OPTIONS

The engine options available in 1965 were the same as 1964, with one exception. The K66 Transistor Ignition System sold much better in 1965 with 3,686 cars being produced with the option. The N03 36-Gallon Fuel Tank option was still rarely bought, with only 41 being sold. The N11 Off-Road Exhaust System also gained in popularity, with a production number of 2,468.

The new addition to the engine option lineup was the N14 Side Mount Exhaust System. These side pipes replaced the conventional exhaust that ran under the car and exited in the rear. With the N14 option, the exhaust pipes ran from the exhaust manifolds, down, and then out through rocker pipes under the door. The pipes contained internal mufflers and turned out at their exit point just in front of the rear wheels. To protect the driver and passenger's legs while entering and exiting, the pipes were covered with slotted heat shields. The side pipes cost $134 and were actually not very popular in their first year. Only 759 cars left the factory with side pipes in 1965.

DRIVELINE

The base transmission for 1965 was still a three-speed manual and was still a rarity. Of the 23,562 1965 Corvettes made, 23,128 came with an optional transmission. The transmission of choice continued to be the $188

A welcomed change came in 1965 when the Corvette was equipped with disc brakes as standard equipment. The brake calipers of the Corvette were far more advanced than most on the road and are very similar to modern performance calipers. Each caliper contained four separate pistons to apply even pressure to the large pads. The brake system still relied on a single-circuit master cylinder. The federal government would eventually mandate a dual-circuit.

M20 four-speed. The manual unit was bolted to 21,107 Corvette engines. The reliable old Powerglide was still available under code M35 and cost $199. It continued to be the only automatic available and in 1965 only 2,021 Powerglide-equipped Corvettes were pro-duced. The $42 G81 Positraction option was added to almost 20,000 Corvettes in 1965 and 1,886 buyers chose the 3.08:1 highway gear for a very reasonable $2. The other gears available were still the 3.36:1, 3.55:1, 3.70:1, 4.11:1, and the 4.56:1.

SUSPENSION, STEERING & BRAKES

While the engine choices and braking system were advancing in 1965, the basic suspension and steering system of the Corvette remained essentially unchanged. The front suspension still carried coil springs and the rear a 9-leaf rear spring. The sway bar arrangement also remained the same with a .75-inch bar in the front and no bar in the rear. The suspension upgrade was also carried over from 1964. Once again, the F40 option was available and upgraded the suspension to stiffer front springs and a 7-leaf rear spring. The F40 also added better shocks, a bigger sway bar in the front and a sway bar in the rear. Although the F40 option cost a mere $37, it was added to only 975 Corvettes in 1965. The steering system also remained the same, and the N40 Power Steering option was still a relatively rare option. Once again, only about 3,000 buyers chose the option. The system rose significantly in price from $75 to $96.

While the new big-block engine took most of the limelight in 1965 there was another performance enhancement just as, or perhaps more, significant—better brakes. Since the C2 was introduced it had retained a relatively antiquated and non-cutting-edge drum brake system. But in 1965 the four-wheel drum brakes disappeared forever from the Corvette's life. Well, *almost* disappeared, but we'll get to that in a bit. While the new brakes did not give the Corvette the brakes of a racecar, they did make stopping a street Corvette a much more sure task. Performance-wise it was probably a more important step than the 50 extra horsepower brought to the table by the new big-block. The standard braking system on the 1965 Corvette was a non-powered system that worked with a single hydraulic line. The master cylinder was still a single circuit unit mounted in the traditional position. Inside, the master cylinder had a 1-inch bore to push the hydraulic fluid through the lines.

The main line was split to the four individual lines running to the calipers. Instead of floating, single, or dual-piston calipers, the 1965 Corvette was equipped with a hard-mounted performance caliper consisting of two pistons per pad for a total of four per caliper. It was certainly an advanced system for any car in 1965. Modern Nextel Cup racecars use a braking system with a very similar design. Although today's racers rely on lighter materials, they still have calipers with four pistons per cylinder that are arranged much the same. The new system provided better braking and eliminated the need for brake system adjustments.

Of course a few new gremlins would occasionally surface. If the car was not driven the bores in the caliper could corrode a bit, leading to leaks at the caliper. Plus, any system with more seals and fittings has more chances to leak. But the problems that arose were well worth the increased stopping ability. Disc brakes were made standard, but it is still possible to come across a 1965 Corvette with drum brakes. Since Chevrolet still had a bunch of drum brakes lying around, some corporate genius decided to offer a $64 credit, under the code J61, for a drum-brake substitution credit. If the option was selected buyers saved a bit of money by replacing the new disc brake system with leftover drum brakes from 1964. Three hundred sixteen poor, misguided souls did so. The J61 was not the only option

The brakes used were not off the shelf, but specifically designed for the performance-oriented Corvette. Both front (left) and rear (right) calipers had four pistons each.

The addition of four-wheel disc brakes meant a new parking brake system. The parking brake consisted of a small set of drum brakes in the rear. The rear rotors had a drum in their center that housed the shoes and hardware.

for Corvette braking. With the drum brakes phased out, the J56 and J65 options, which featured the sintered metallic pads, disappeared. However, the J50 power brake option remained on the RPO list at $43. Like the powered drum brakes, the system relied on a large vacuum chamber, mounted on the master cylinder, to assist the driver's effort. Corvettes equipped with the J50 option had a completely different master cylinder and the system was plumbed a bit differently. The master cylinder featured dual reservoirs and dual lines to feed the front calipers and the rear. The system was a bit safer, as a leak in one line would not leave the driver without brakes.

The standard wheel for the 1965 Corvette was a 15-inch steel wheel with a width of five inches and a five-lug pattern. The wheel was once again trimmed with a new wheel cover. While much of the Corvette stayed the same year to year, the wheel covers were often changed. For 1965, the cover had six slots. They were wider than the eight slots on the 1964 wheel cover. The slots were accented around their inner perimeter with a charcoal finish. The center of the wheel cover had the fake spinner with the crossed-flag emblem on a black background.

The P48 Cast Aluminum Knock-off Wheels were still available in 1965 and still expensive at $322 a set. Because of this, and their lingering questionable reputation, Chevrolet sold only 1,116 sets in 1965. There was a major change in the Corvette's rubber in 1965. The tire size was changed from 6.70 x 15 to 7.75 x 15. The additional width was welcomed both for handling and traction when trying to

accelerate with the more and more powerful engines. A number of tire companies supplied the Corvette factory. They included Goodyear, Firestone, B.F. Goodrich, General, and U.S. Royal. The option list showed three tire choices in 1965. By far the most popular was the P92 Whitewalls, which were put on about 82 percent of the 1965s produced. The P91 Blackwall Tires were also still available and joined by a new tire option—the T01 Goldwall Tires, which featured a gold stripe around the tire in place of a white stripe. The Goldwall Tires were the most expensive of the optional tires with a set costing $50. Only 989 sets were mounted on Corvettes in 1965.

1965 SUMMARY

The results of the sales year were much like those of 1964, and while they were not yet to the 30,000 mark, they were still good. Coupe sales were down a little over 100 cars but still healthy at 8,186 units. Convertible sales, on the other hand, grew to 15,376 units, up almost 1,500 from 1964. The revenue to Chevrolet, based on list prices, was $35,371,706 for coupe sales, $63,133,856 for convertible sales, and $18,336,296 for option sales. This meant that the Corvette line added $116,841,858 to the Chevrolet coffers in 1965.

The knock-off aluminum wheels were still available under code P48. The spinner nut had the loosening direction engraved in the side.

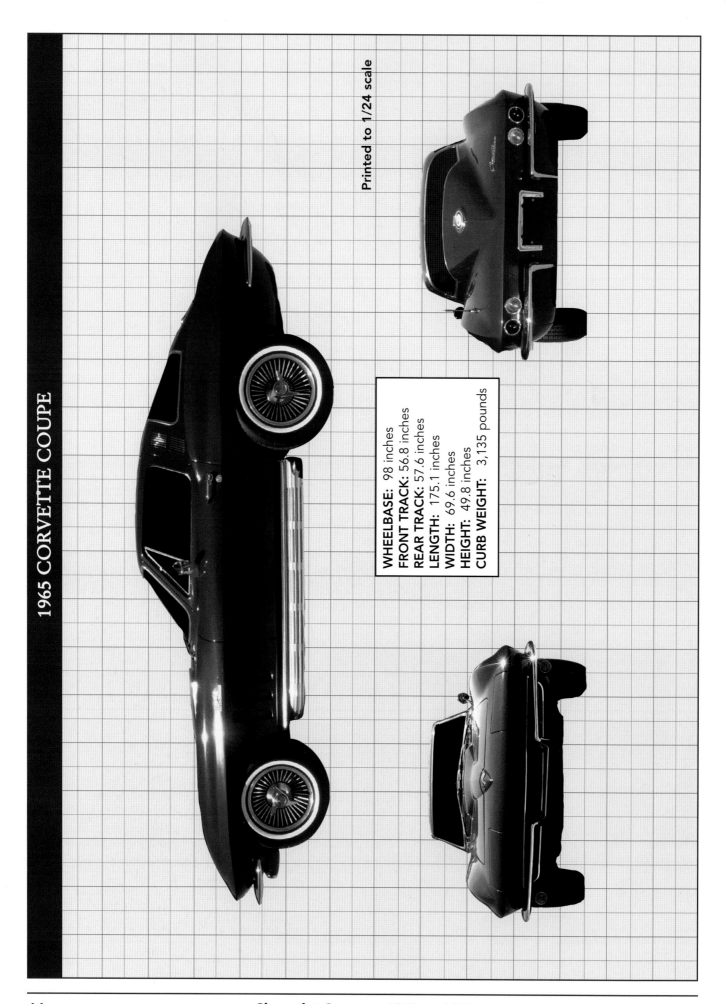

1965 CORVETTE COUPE

WHEELBASE: 98 inches
FRONT TRACK: 56.8 inches
REAR TRACK: 57.6 inches
LENGTH: 175.1 inches
WIDTH: 69.6 inches
HEIGHT: 49.8 inches
CURB WEIGHT: 3,135 pounds

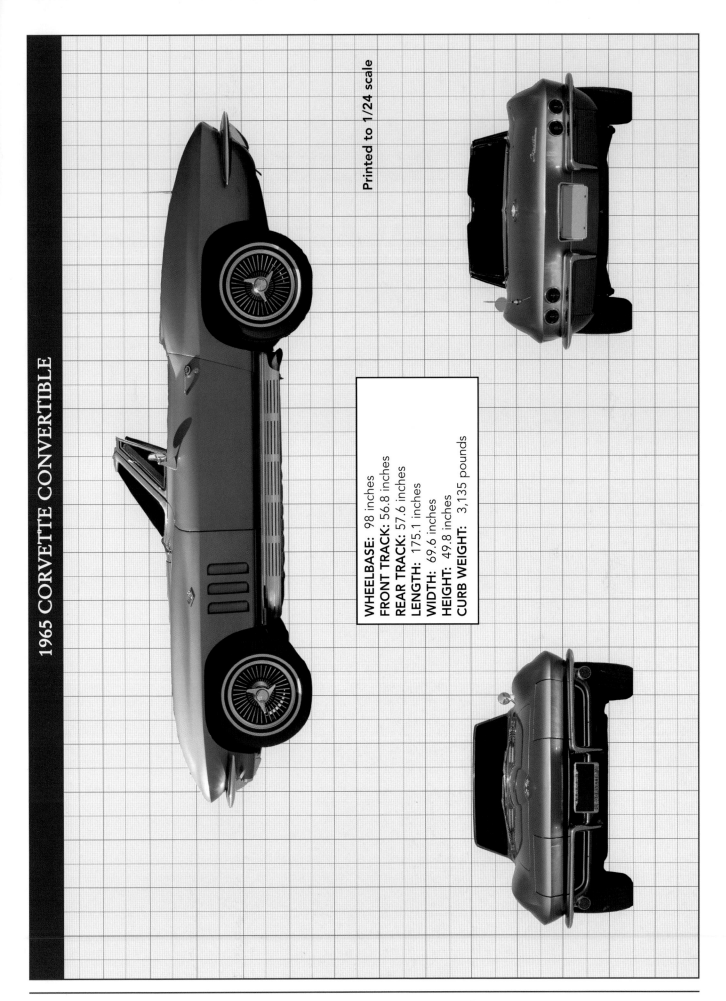

1965 CORVETTE CONVERTIBLE

Printed to 1/24 scale

WHEELBASE: 98 inches
FRONT TRACK: 56.8 inches
REAR TRACK: 57.6 inches
LENGTH: 175.1 inches
WIDTH: 69.6 inches
HEIGHT: 49.8 inches
CURB WEIGHT: 3,135 pounds

1966 CORVETTE

When the 1966 sales year began, the Corvette platform was finally getting where the factory (and the public) wanted it and changes made to the matured chassis and body were insignificant. The brakes had taken a grand leap the year before and required no major changes. The interior also saw few changes, receiving only a couple of safety and comfort items. The biggest change in 1966 was in the engine department. The 1966 option list showed that the guard had truly been changed. From 1963 to 1965 all of the engine choices, with the exception of the L78 introduced in 1965, were variants of the small-block 327. A total of five versions of the 327 were available during those three years. But in 1966 the move to big-blocks for the highest performance engines was complete. The result for the performance enthusiast was staggering. With bugs worked out and the big motors available, 1966 saw production of the nastiest Corvettes to date—nasty in a good way.

The price of a Corvette actually went down in 1966. The price of the coupe dropped $26 from $4,321 to $4,295, while the price of the convertible dropped $22 from $4,106 to $4,084.

By 1966 the C2 was a mature automotive platform. Small changes had been made every year since 1963, and 1966 was the same. The 1966's body was very much like the 1965's with the major changes occurring under the hood.

Blue continued to be a popular color choice with buyers in 1966. In 1966, 6,022 Corvettes were painted Nassau Blue making it by far the most popular color. The soft convertible top could be supplemented with the C07 Auxiliary Hardtop for $231. In 1966, 8,463 of the 17,762 convertible buyers ordered the top, which attached to the car using the same latches as the soft top.

Even in soft colors like Sunfire Yellow the Corvette kept its aggressive appearance. Only 2,339 cars left the factory in 1966 with this color.

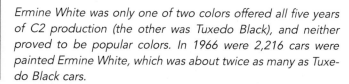

Ermine White was only one of two colors offered all five years of C2 production (the other was Tuxedo Black), and neither proved to be popular colors. In 1966 were 2,216 cars were painted Ermine White, which was about twice as many as Tuxedo Black cars.

While some things changed over the years, one that didn't was the body's wonderful lines. With the exception of hoods and the openings behind the front wheels, there were no major body changes to the C2 during the five years of its production.

Soft tops were still available in white, black, and beige in 1966. Convertible sales outpaced coupe sales again in 1966. By year's end, 17,762 convertibles and 9,958 coupes left the assembly plant for a record total of 27,720 Corvettes.

CHASSIS & BODY

The mature C2 chassis and body received few changes for the 1966 production year. The frames used in 1965 were identical, with the exception of the serial numbers and factory markings. The body of the 1966 also stayed much the same and was almost identical to the 1965. While the body stayed the same, there were once again color changes, which included more overall choices. The color chart in 1966 featured 10 colors, up from eight in 1965. The perennial Tuxedo Black and Ermine White colors were, of course, still available. Rally Red and Milano Maroon, introduced in 1965, were also carried over to 1966. All of the other shades available in 1965 were dropped in favor of new ones. The choice of blues was expanded to three: Marina Blue, Laguna Blue, and Trophy Blue. Mosport Green, Sunfire Yellow, and Silver Pearl rounded out the color choices. Surprisingly, the most popular color for 1966 was not Tuxedo Black or Rally Red, but Marina Blue, with 6,100 cars being so painted. Perhaps even more surprisingly, Milano Maroon was the second most popular at 3,799. The rest of the numbers included Rally Red (3,366), Silver Pearl (2,967), Sunfire Yellow (2,339), Mosport Green (2,311), Ermine White (2,120), Laguna Blue (2,054), and Trophy Blue (1,463). The biggest surprise was the least common color in 1966. There were only 1,190 1966 Corvettes to leave the factory with Tuxedo Black paint.

The Corvette had a new grille in 1966. The grille used in '65 had horizontal elements, but the '66 had a grille with small rectangular elements. The front edges of the new grille were finished in chrome with the interior elements having a matte grey finish.

The big-block hood that was introduced with the 396 was used in 1966 to cover the new 427. The grille featured slotted air intakes on each side of the hood's hump.

The quick and easy convertible system remained the same throughout C2 production. The hideaway top could be released, folded, and stored in less than a minute. The center latch released the side latches so that the door could be opened.

BODY OPTIONS

As in previous years, the A01 Soft Ray Tinted Glass (all windows) and the A02 Soft Ray Tinted Glass (windshield only) were still available for $15 and $10, respectively. Convertible owners got a bit of security and made the winter months more bearable with the C07 Auxiliary Hardtop. The top dropped in price $5 to $231 and came with 8,463 of the 17,762 1966 Corvette convertibles produced. A new item on the 1966 option list was the V74 Traffic Hazard Lamp Switch. When this option was ordered the buyer got the same type of hazard light activation that is standard on all modern cars. The option cost $11 and was installed on 5,764 1966s. Nineteen sixty-six was the only year that the V74 option was available. Hazard lights became standard in 1967.

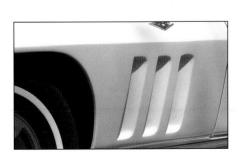

The side "gills" behind the fenders introduced in 1965 continued in 1966. It was their last year, as '67 brought a new design. These side features are the quickest way to nail a C2 down as being a '65 or '66. From there, closer examination is usually required to tell which year it is.

On cars equipped with the standard exhaust system the tail pipes had chrome tips that exited the rear body panel through chrome bezels.

Side-pipe-equipped cars had no need of the aperture in the rear panel; therefore, it was left solid.

The chrome license bracket was centered between the rear bumpers and contained a recessed light in the top.

The gas cap made its yearly transformation to a new style in 1966. This time it placed the crossed flags on a small circle surrounded by a sunburst pattern of tight ridges. The door kept its chrome frame and hinge. The inside of the gas filler door was unchanged from previous years. A plastic boot with a drain tube surrounded the filler neck. This allowed gas overflow or rainwater to be drained away from the filler neck.

The Corvette's glass came standard with no tinting, but it could be added at a very reasonable price. The A01 option added Soft Ray Tint to all of the car's windows for only $15. The A02 option added tinting to the windshield only for $10. Over 75 percent of the '66s produced had one of the two options.

The door handle remained t same as 1965 models and v flush mounted to the side of t door.

INTERIOR

The Corvette interior, once again, was little changed from the year before. Like the rest of the car it had slowly matured and required little attention. While the changes were few, the 1966 interior does have its differences.

The seat covers underwent another stitching change. For 1966 the seats had eight horizontal panels on the back and seven on the seat bottom. Two different seatbelt buckles were produced for the 1966 Corvettes. The first had a flat cover with a silver bowtie and a pull-type release system. The second had a recessed release button with a blue bowtie surrounding the word "Chevrolet."

Under the seats the molded carpet that was introduced in 1965 was carried over and used again in 1966. Because of the engine changes, a few changes that affected gauges. Cars equipped with a base engine or the L36 still had tachometers that redlined at 5,500 rpm.

Cars with an L79 boasted a 6,000-rpm redline, while those with the L72 redlined at 6,500 rpm. All water gauges had a 250-degree maximum number and the oil pressure gauges were rated at 60 psi. A few cars with L36s were reported to have left the factory with 80-psi oil pressure gauges. For 1966 the

colors choices for the interior also changed a bit. The available solid colors included black, red, blue, Saddle, silver, and green like the year before. All of the colors were available with leather or vinyl seats, with the exception of green.

While green leather seats had been available in 1965, they were not available

There were seven solid interior color choices in 1966, including black, red, blue, maroon, Saddle, green, and silver.

One of the most striking Corvette interiors was the two-tone interior. In 1966 the two-tone choices were black and white or blue and white. This blue and white interior has been matched with an Ermine White body.

The same gauge layout was used throughout the C2 production run. Whether the car had a base engine or the most powerful optional engine, the driver was rewarded with a full complement of information.

Throughout its existence, the C2 had many amenities as standard equipment that were options on other cars. The windshield washer system is an example. The wiper knob featured a center pushbutton that activated the washer pump.

The under-dash pull handle parking brake was used from 1963 to 1966.

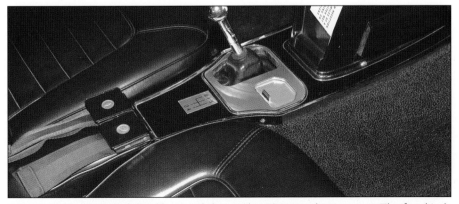

There were two seatbelt buckles used during the 1966 production year. The first buckle's face was color matched to the car's interior with a circular silver button featuring a silver Chevrolet bowtie.

The second buckle had a brushed metal face with a square black button that also featured the bowtie. The bowtie on this buckle was blue with a chrome border and had "Chevrolet" imprinted in block letters.

The interior's control knobs changed a bit in 1966. The previous knobs had been all chrome, but the new knobs featured a recessed face that was finished in black.

The white seats and door panels of the two-tone interiors were good looking and stylish, but hard to keep clean.

The jack storage was in the well just behind the passenger's seat. Corvettes made use of a scissor jack, which could get under the low-slung car (even lower with a flat tire).

The door panels were carried over from the '65 model. While they were very striking, they were difficult to keep clean and the quickest to show wear.

Nineteen sixty-six was the last year with the door lock at the back top of the door panel. It was soon moved forward in order to make it a bit more accessible.

The door panels used on coupes were like those used on convertibles. The inside frame of the window was pained black to match this black interior.

The double-hump dash top remained the same in 1966. The defroster duct is visible just forward of the radio speaker cover. The passenger's hump still featured the "hold on" cutout, but '66 would be its last year.

in 1966. A new color, Bright Blue, was added for 1966 and was available with leather or vinyl seats. The only other choice in interior combinations was the white and blue two-tone interior. Like the green seats, the leather option in this choice was dropped and in 1966 it was only available with vinyl seats.

INTERIOR OPTIONS

The usual suspects were still around in the interior option lineup but in 1966 were joined by a couple of newcomers. Leather seats were still not very popular, being installed in just 7 percent of the 1966 Corvettes produced. Air conditioning and power windows were also not very common. Air and power windows were added to only 13 percent of the 1966s. The teak

The U69 AM-FM Radio was still a popular option in 1966, although it was very expensive ($199). The radio was shipped with a tag informing buyers of the reception they could hope to receive with this relatively new piece of technology.

steering wheel and telescoping steering wheel were added to 14 and 13 percent, respectively. The new items on the option list were the A82 headrest and the A85 shoulder belts. The headrest was a slim unit that cost $42 and was added to 1,033 (3.7 percent) 1966s. The benefit of shoulder belts was still not fully recognized by consumers in 1966. Only 37 1966 Corvettes were produced with the $26 option.

When air conditioning was added to the C2, the center console changed a bit. An extra vent was added at the top, as were the two AC system control knobs. Below the clock the center dash was the same as non-AC cars.

ENGINE & DRIVETRAIN

In 1966 the biggest changes to the Corvette again centered on the powertrain. Both the engine and transmission lineups underwent significant changes that would further delight the performance enthusiasts. The shakeup would again be centered on the big-block line. The life of the 396 was short lived. Its first year, 1965, was also its last. The engine was the bridge that carried Corvette owners from the 327-ci engines to the 427-ci engines. In 1966 the 396 was replaced with the new 427-ci engine. It was by far the largest engine ever offered in a Corvette to date.

The reason for its existence is probably as much due to Ford as to Chevrolet. Ford 427s were appearing in Cobras, and Chevrolet wanted to keep its stranglehold on the American-built sports car market. As Chevrolet made the move to "cubic inches for horsepower," the number of engine options actually dropped from 1965. During the previous year's sales season the factory offered five engine options above the base 327 engine. In 1966 the number of optional engines would drop to three.

The base engine for the Corvette was still the venerable small-block 327 — but things had changed. As mentioned in the previous chapter, the optional L75 engine had been discontinued. It was no coincidence that the 1966 base engine had the same horsepower and torque ratings as the discontinued L75. While there were a few minor differences between the base engine and the 1965 L75, they were much the same. The 1966

The 327-ci small-block continued its reign in 1966; however, Chevrolet offered only the base 327 and one optional version of the engine. The base engine's block, heads, valve covers, and intake manifold were painted in Chevrolet Orange.

For the first time in C2 history the base engine was the most common engine. Much of this was due to the base engine growing from 250 to 300 horsepower.

The base engine didn't have the fancy aluminum valve covers of the high-performance small-blocks and had to do with stamped covers painted Chevrolet Orange. But its 300 horsepower and 360 ft-lbs of torque were plenty for the 9,755 who elected to stay with the base engine.

The only optional 327 was the 350-hp L79. This engine cost buyers an additional $105 and provided them with 50 more horsepower than the base engine. Of the 27,720 1966 Corvettes purchased, 7,591 had an L79 under the hood, making it the most popular optional engine in 1966.

The L79 was decked out with finned aluminum valve covers and an open-element air cleaner. Like all Corvette engines, it was shipped with the complex array of ignition shielding.

Judges always seem to debate, so "factory" and "original" can be slippery slopes. With the soaring values of C2s it is important when doing a restoration to get the details right. The overspray on this manifold is an attempt to reproduce what occurred at the factory.

The ignition shielding was still around in 1966. While it helped eliminate radio interference and protect ignition components, it was never a favorite with mechanics who had to remove all the components to perform a simple tune-up. The task was made easier by the use of butterfly nuts, which usually meant the shields could be removed without tools.

The thermostat housing was a cast unit on the L79. It was complemented with a chrome oil filler that tilted forward.

base engine was rated at 300 horsepower at 5,000 rpm and 360 ft-lbs of torque at 3,200 rpm. The engine still had 10.50:1 compression, but now carried many parts previously used on the L75. These included improved valvetrain components and, for the first time, a Holley carburetor. The base engine still redlined at 5,500 rpm. By bumping the horsepower of the base engine Chevrolet made an attempt to eliminate the need for a "first step" option small-block. They were successful, as 9,755 1966 Corvettes had the base engine as opposed to 3,234, which was the average base engine production from 1963 to 1965. For the first time in C2 history, the base engine was the most common engine in a model year.

The only other small-block choice in 1966 was listed under a new code—L79. This engine was a traditionally carbureted 327 rated at 350 horsepower at 5,800 rpm and 360 ft-lbs of torque at 3,600 rpm. Chevrolet accepted that there was a big block of buyers (pun intended) who wanted to stay with a small-block engine. The optional small-block was still a couple of hundred pounds lighter and made very good power. The new L79 was rated at 350 horsepower at 5,800 rpm and 360 ft-lbs of torque at 3,600 rpm. The L79 was built with 11.00:1 compression, was fitted with a Holley four-barrel, and retained the more "user friendly" hydraulic lifters. In 1966 the L79 redlined at 6,000 rpm. The L79 was the most popular engine in 1966 with 7,591 Corvettes leaving the factory with one. At only $105 it was a cheap way to get a 50-hp increase over the base 327.

1966 Big-Blocks

Visualize a small cardboard box that's 2 x 5 x 1 inches. Or just pick up an average paperback book. Its volume is roughly the difference in volume between the 327-ci V-8 and the 427-ci V-8, which is, of course, 100 cubic inches. Cut the book up into eight pieces and that's how much more displacement each cylinder received. It may not seem like much when you're holding it in your hand, but it sure seems like a lot when it's under your right foot. Just as Corvette enthusiasts were getting used to the sight of the huge 396 engine introduced in 1965 it was gone. The good news was that taking its place were even bigger engines with 427 cubic inches. The first engine offered in the 427 lineup was the L36. Boring the cylinders of the huge block to 4.000 inches and stretching the stroke to 4.125 inches achieved its 427-ci displacement. Compression was kept to a reasonable 10.25:1 and hydraulic lifters were used.

The 396 was gone from the Corvette lineup after only one year. General Motors' 400-ci limit was relaxed for '66 and two variants of the 427 were added to the option list.

Air conditioning could be added to any Corvette engine. The large Frigidaire® compressor was mounted high in the right side of the engine. Air conditioning was not the standard as it is today and only 10 percent of all C2s produced had the system.

The aluminum coolant expansion tank was located in the right side fender. The expansion tank held any coolant that was pushed out of the cooling system where it was stored until it could be drawn back in when the car cooled.

The simple painted valve covers were huge on the 427. There were two 427s for 1966—the L36 and the L72. The engines were nearly equal in popularity with both selling roughly 500 units.

The C2 had a mechanical clutch as opposed to a hydraulic clutch. The pivot point in the clutch system was this bar that ran from the engine to the side of the engine well. The bar's connection to the clutch pedal is visible in the bar's outer end.

With a redline of 5,500 rpm the engine was first rated at 400 horsepower, but the rating was later dropped to 390 horsepower. The 390 horsepower was achieved at 5,200 rpm. The big difference made by the 427 was in the torque. The L36 made a ground-thumping 460 ft-lbs of torque at 3,600 rpm. Both numbers were most likely understated. Insurance companies were beginning to catch on and the factory was at times reluctant to let them know just how much power they were putting on the streets. The L36 listed for $181 and had the same basic look as all Corvette engines with the exception of size. The valve covers looked like you could play a game of tennis on them. The engine had a chrome air-filter housing with horsepower and engine size decals, a Holley four-barrel, an aluminum intake manifold, and painted valve covers. The L36 was a popular choice with 1966 Corvette buyers. It was very reasonably priced and by year's end 5,116 had left

the factory, meaning that 18 percent of the cars produced in 1966 had an L36 engine.

It meant an extra $312 above the base engine and $131 above the cost of the L36—and many could not resist. While the L36 was popular with buyers, it was surpassed by the engine that occu-

pied the power throne for 1966—the L72. Chevrolet used the same bore and stroke, but with the addition of mechanical lifters and by boosting compression up to 11.0:1, the Chevrolet engine gurus were able to push horsepower well over the 400 mark. The L72 used a Holley four-barrel for fuel delivery and the redline was upped to 6,500 rpm. For unknown reasons the engine carried a 450-hp rating when first released, but the rating was dropped to 425 horsepower later in the production run. The engine was pricey, but 5,258 people ordered one, meaning that almost 20 percent of the 1966s produced had an L72 engine.

ENGINE OPTIONS

In 1966 the engine options were the same as in 1965 and consisted of the 36-gallon fuel tank, the off-road exhaust, and the side-pipe exhaust. The only differences were that the 36-gallon tank dropped $4 in price, the off-road exhaust dropped $1, and the side pipes dropped $3. The N14 side pipes were much more popular during the 1966 sales year. Sales of the units rose from 759 in 1965 to 3,617 in 1966. The K66 Transistor Ignition System continued to be offered costing $73 and was added to 7,146 engines. A new item on the engine option list was the K19 Air Injection Reactor. While this item sounded like a performance item, it was not. In fact, it was much the opposite. Also known as the smog pump, the Air Injection Reactor was mounted on the front of the engine much in the same way as the alternator. The unit pumped air into the exhaust and was driven by a belt, which meant it was a dead horsepower drain. The unit was mandatory on cars sold in

Nineteen sixty-six was the last year of the single-circuit brake system. Used from '63 to '66, the system relied on one hydraulic line from the master cylinder to power the brakes on all four corners. A failure in the master cylinder's single piston or in the line meant that the driver only had the emergency brake to stop the car.

The wheel covers for 1966 were a new design, just as they were in 1963, 1964, and 1965. It kept the center "fake" spinner nut, but the spokes were changed to create more of a "mag" wheel look. The circular surface behind the spokes had a frosted silver finish.

The aluminum wheels with the knock-off system made their last appearance on the '66 Corvette. The wheels were added to 1,194 1966s. The gold stripe tire was introduced in 1965 and discontinued after 1966. They were the most expensive tire choice in 1966, with a set costing $46.

California, a state that was well ahead of the rest of the nation in pollution control. The K19 set California buyers back $44 and was added to 2,380 1966 Corvettes.

DRIVELINE

The choice of transmissions was also expanded in 1966. Within the manual lineup the M20 was still available, but production dropped from over 20,000 units in 1965 to just over 10,000 in 1966. The reason for the drop was the introduction of the M21. The M21 was also a four-speed, but featured a close ratio throw, which was much more performance oriented. Chevrolet sold the M21 for the same price as the M20 and, as a result, almost 14,000 were installed. The other transmission available in 1967 was the new M22 heavy-duty, close ratio four-speed, which became affectionately known as "the rock crusher." A 1966 Corvette with an M22 is a rare commodity. Factory records indicate that only 15 cars were shipped with the beefiest of the gearboxes. It is surprising because the transmission was only about $50 more than an M20 or M21. Positraction was still a popular option, with 24,056 1966 Corvettes receiving the $42 drivetrain upgrade. The G91 Special Highway Axle option, which put a 3.08:1 gear in the rear end, was removed from the option list in 1966, but the gear was still available. Buyers could still choose between six rear gear choices in 1966. The gear ratios available were 3.08:1, 3.36:1, 3.55:1, 3.70:1, 4.11:1, and 4.56:1.

SUSPENSION, STEERING & BRAKES

The base suspension and steering remained more or less unchanged from the 1965 Corvette. The only significant change to the Corvette suspension in 1966 was on the option list. For the first time the performance suspension upgrade was listed under the code F41. The package itself did not change much and still equipped the car with a stiffer front coil spring, a stiffer 7-leaf rear leaf spring, and sway bars in the front and rear. The option listed for a mere $36, but was only added to 2,705 of the 27,720 Corvettes produced in 1966. Steering was still made easier with the N40 Power Steering option. The option sold better than in 1965, with the number of power steering-equipped cars rising from 3,235 in 1965 to 5,611 in 1966. The disc brake system introduced in 1965 remained unchanged for the 1966 production run. The only new news in the area of brakes was the appearance of the J56 Special Heavy Duty Brakes. The option cost a whopping $342 and replaced the standard brake system. Only 382 Corvettes received the option in 1966.

In 1966 the base wheel was once again the same as the previous years and once again the wheel cover was changed. The 1966 cover still had the fake spinner bolt, but now featured five thick spokes. The spokes, center, and rim of the cover were finished in chrome and were accented with a matte surface underneath.

The P48 option continued to be the only factory wheel option and actually dropped $6 in price for 1966. Production of the wheels remained about the same, with 1,194 sets being sold. In 1966 the standard tire was still a 7.75 x 15 Blackwall. The P92 option still provided a set of whitewalls for $31 and 17,969 buyers once again made this the most popular style. The P91 option was discontinued after the 1965 sales season, making the T01 Goldwall Tires the only other tire option. Goodyear, Firestone, B.F. Goodrich, General, and U.S. Royal continued to be the Corvette tire suppliers.

1966 SUMMARY

When 1966 drew to a close, a record 27,720 Corvettes had left the factory. Production was split between 9,958 coupes and 17,762 convertibles. Since the coupe's introduction in 1963, when sales had been split about 50/50 between coupes and convertibles, the convertibles sold at about a 2-to-1 margin over the coupes. The total number of Corvettes sold was still short of 30,000, but based on the list price, represented revenue of $115,309,618. Option sales added $22,566,300, for a total of $137,875,918. The Corvette program was in fine shape, and as buyers gobbled up the 1966 Corvettes the guys back at Corvette headquarters were looking to the future. The C2 program still had a way to go, but within the walls of Chevrolet, drawings, models, and prototypes were slowly coming together into a design that would mean the end of the C2.

While the Grand Sport era was over it was not the end of the Corvette racing effort. Many privateers raced the car with limited success. It was once again Roger Penske who took the Corvette to the top, this time in a form much closer to stock. By 1966 the road version of the Corvette was upgraded to disc brakes and was no longer limited to small block engines. The 396 introduced in 1965 was scrapped after only one year in favor of the 427. In 1966 Corvette was available with two new 427 cubic inch big-blocks. The smallest was rated at 390 horsepower and the largest was rated at 425 horsepower. Zora Duntov and his team of engineers worked on a higher output version of the new 427 during 1964 and 1965. This secret engine was coded L-88. Zora wanted this engine to only be available to certified racing teams. The engine was scheduled to be offered in the newly revised 1967 C3 Corvette. Production problems delayed introduction of the revised Corvette until 1968. So Zora decided to make the engine available in limited quantities in the hastily revised 1967 C2 Corvette. Zora quietly installed one of these engines in a red 66 Corvette coupe in November of 1965. He made it available to successful Grand Sport racer Roger Penske. The 1966 coupe was produced using the COPO system. Under the title of Central Office Production Order, cars could be produced in forms not available through the standard ordering process. The car created under the COPO was a red '66 coupe with the L88 engine and TI ignition, the off-road exhaust, an M22 four-speed, a special 2.73:1 Positraction rear gear, and a 36-gallon fuel tank. The car rode on an F41 suspension and had the J56 heavy-duty brakes. Inside, the car had a teak-wood steering wheel, a telescoping column, and was built with radio and heater delete. Upon completion the car was sold to Roger Penske. The car was equipped with a cowl induction hood that opened near the base of the windshield. It was built in December 1965. This was the first L-88 produced.

The car was picked up at the St. Louis plant by Corvette driver Dick Guldstrand. He drove it to Penske's shop in Pennsylvania in freezing weather to get it ready for the 1966 24 Hours of Daytona. Since the car had no heater Guldstrand was given a blanket by a Corvette plant worker to stay warm. With Duntov's input, Penske assembled a top-notch team to prepare the car for its first trial. It was the first time that the Daytona road race would run 24 hours like Le Mans. When the team arrived at the track the car was wickedly fast in the GT category, setting blistering laps in practice. Just before the race the factory sent a fresh L88 engine that was said to be rated at about 540 horsepower. The team gleefully dropped it in. When the green flag dropped the car raced well, but adversity was to come. In the middle of the night Guldstrand plowed into the back of a triumph and knocked the front of the car off. During pit repairs a mechanic accidentaly stuck a screwdriver through the radiator. This incident happened around 4 AM, which happened to be one of the coldest winters in Florida's history. It was around 18 degrees when the radiator was damaged. Penske sent the car back out with the damaged radiator while the crew looked for a replacement radiator. The crew found a black 427 Corvette in the parking lot and they quickly removed the car's radiator and left the owner a

Penske's 1966 racer was much more kin to the Corvettes roaming the streets than it was to the Grand Sports. The car was built under the COPO system, but had options that were available to any who bought a 1966 Corvette, including the 36-gallon fuel tank, the F41 suspension, and the J56 brakes. It also had the telescoping steering column and teak steering wheel. (Bill Erdman Photography)

note on his windshield about their dirty deed. The new radiator was installed and the car was sent back into competition. Shortly after its return to competition, it was black flagged by the race officials for not having any headlights. Corvette engineer Gib Hufsteader taped flashlights to the front fenders in place of headlights. When the car went back out on the track the driver relied on a Ferrari team car's taillights to help navigate the track in the darkness. The car had to pit for new flashlight batteries every fifteen minutes until daylight.

Despite the problems, the banged up '66 won the GT class and finished 11th overall, thrilling the team and allowing the guy in the parking lot with no radiator to finally go home. The car backed up its Daytona performance the next month at Sebring. With Sunoco as the team's new sponsor the car was painted the company colors—blue with yellow trim. The car again won the GT class, this time with much less drama, and finished ninth overall in the 12-hour endurance race. Penske sold the car after Sebring and began racing a Lola T-70 with an L-88 engine in the Can-Am series. Like the Grand Sports, the '66 survived its racing days and after a pristine restoration by Corvette Repair in Valley Stream, New York, joins the ranks of the most desirable and valuable midyear Corvettes alive.

The Penske '66 had a short but impressive run, winning its class in the 1966 24 Hours of Daytona and the 12-hour race at Sebring a month later. (Bill Erdman Photography)

Perhaps the most impressive element of this '66 coupe was its engine. This car was the first Corvette to receive the L88 version of the 427. The guys at the factory who put the prototype L-88 engine into this car claimed it produced 540 horsepower at Daytona. (Bill Erdman Photography)

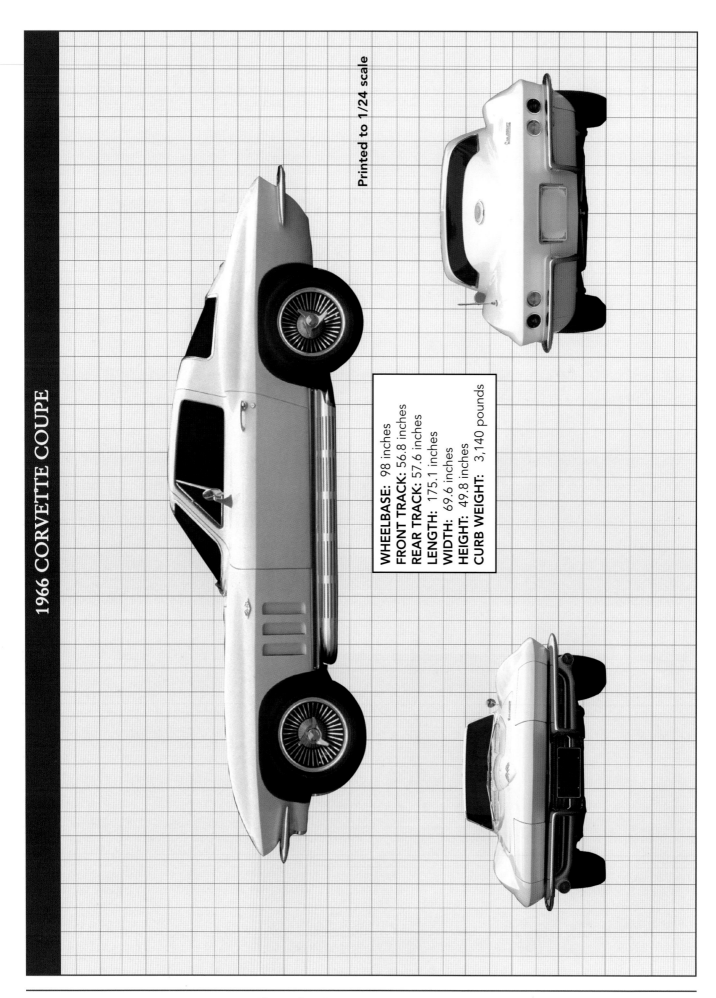

1966 CORVETTE COUPE

Printed to 1/24 scale

WHEELBASE: 98 inches
FRONT TRACK: 56.8 inches
REAR TRACK: 57.6 inches
LENGTH: 175.1 inches
WIDTH: 69.6 inches
HEIGHT: 49.8 inches
CURB WEIGHT: 3,140 pounds

1966 CORVETTE CONVERTIBLE

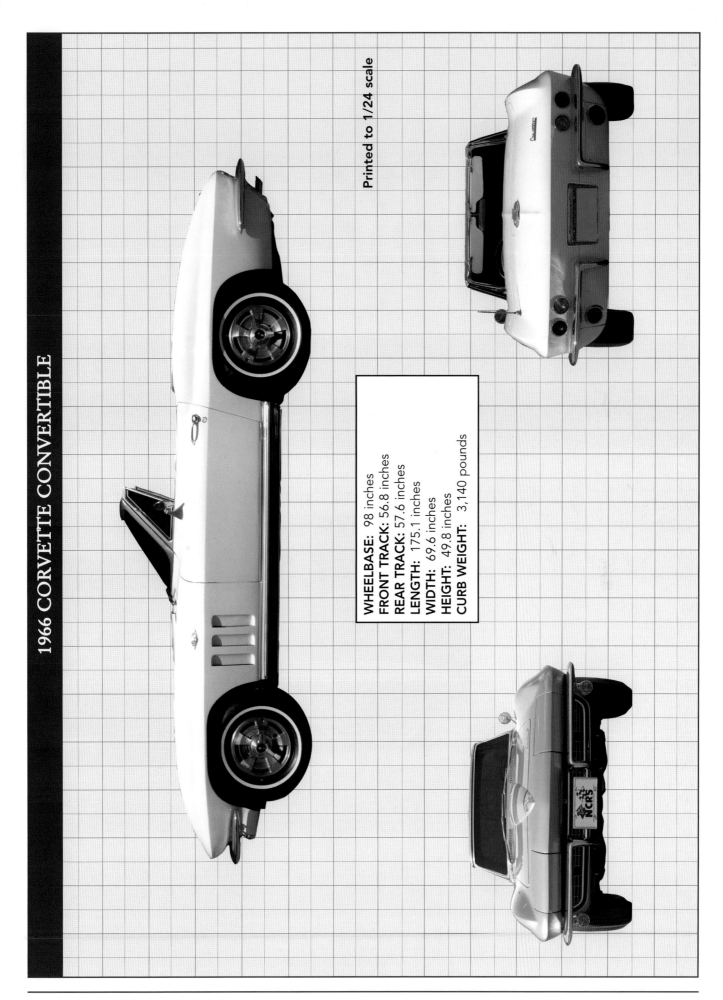

Printed to 1/24 scale

WHEELBASE: 98 inches
FRONT TRACK: 56.8 inches
REAR TRACK: 57.6 inches
LENGTH: 175.1 inches
WIDTH: 69.6 inches
HEIGHT: 49.8 inches
CURB WEIGHT: 3,140 pounds

A funny thing happened on the way to the C3 Corvette. In the mid 1960s, the car wars between manufacturers were as hot as ever. Chevrolet, Ford, and Chrysler were all increasing their lines of performance parts, creating the glory years of the American muscle car. When it came to design and engineering during this period, the feeling was if you were standing still you were going backwards. The Corvette had a bit of an advantage in body development. First off, it was the only American two-seat performance machine that was mass-produced. Ford and Chrysler had no platform in direct competition. Added to that was the fact that other cars' steel body panels were pressed out of sheet steel using expensive molds mounted on expensive presses. This process carried high startup and overhead costs that could only be made up with high-volume production runs so that each car could carry a fraction of the startup cost burden. The Corvette, on the other hand, used much less expensive molds to form the body panels.

While making the body was as labor intensive as ever, the startup cost on a

Chevrolet originally had plans to release the next generation Corvette in 1967. Its inability to meet the schedule resulted in what many believe to be the greatest Corvette ever created. Coupes were well outnumbered in '67 as convertible sales reached 14,436—outpacing coupe sales by nearly a 2-to-1 margin. At year's end the total sales numbers fell short of those of '66, dropping to 22,940.

new shape was not as horrendous and the labor cost could be passed along to the customer. The boys in the design department had been preparing the "next" Corvette in the mid 1960s and were itching to get it into production.

At a distance the 1967 looked much like the 1963 that began the C2 run, but differences had accumulated throughout the car over the years. The process of change did not stop after 1966, even though the 1967 was a stopgap car used until the C3 was ready.

Blues were always popular on midyear Corvettes. In 1967, 9,627 of the Corvettes produced were painted in one of the three shades of blue offered. This two-owner Elkhart Blue '67 is back in Alabama with the original owner after a dozen years with the second owner in Texas.

From this angle it's hard to tell whether this car is a 1967, 1966, or 1965 model. During that period little changed on the base car's nose, hood, and roof.

Initially, the goal was to have the C3 ready for the 1967 sales year, but the effort was not able to keep up with the plan. As a result, the 1967 Corvette would be the last C2 instead of the first C3. This was a good thing. Many feel that the 1967 is the greatest C2 and possibly the greatest of all the Corvette models ever built. The chassis and body had four years of production to have all of the bugs worked out, the suspension was tried and true, and the engine lineup was expanded and ranged from impressive at the bottom to insane at the top.

With a few options the 1967 Corvette could really change its look. While this '67 is painted the same Elkhart Blue color as the stately small-block coupe featured earlier, the look of the car is very different. With the addition of a convertible top, the big-block's new hood, side pipes, aluminum wheels, and red stripe tires, the look has changed from stately to stylishly aggressive with the top up or down. Convertible tops were still available in black and white, but beige was dropped in 1967 and blue was added.

If stately or stylishly aggressive were not enough, the buyer could go all-out and make the '67 downright mean. This coupe has the same big-block hood, side pipes, aluminum wheels, and red stripe tires, but has been sheathed in Rally Red paint, making it downright noticeable. Rally Red was carried over from 1965, but there were not as many little red Corvettes that year as one might think. Only 2,341 of the 22,940 cars produced in 1967 were Rally Red, making it the fourth most popular color.

CHASSIS & BODY

The only significant change to the frame of the 1967 was the mounting structure for the parking brake assembly. The primary bracket was welded to the crossmember on the 1967 model. The hole used on the previous parking brake was also removed from the crossmember. Since the guys at the factory were busy designing and tooling up for the new model of Corvette, the 1967's chassis and body understandably went through a few changes.

One very noticeable change to the body for 1967 was to the slots behind the front wheel wells. The three vertical openings used in 1965 and 1966 were replaced with a new design. The 1967 had a single opening divided into five slots. Instead of being truly vertical like the earlier design, the 1967 openings tilted a bit. The new design closely resembled gills, further cementing the stingray look.

The big-block hood was changed in 1967. The now famous "Stinger" hood was a parting gift from the designers responsible for the C2. The very aggressive style had a large, rectangular hump at the rear of the hood that transitioned into the forward running peak on all Corvettes. The hump and peak were painted black on most colors and red or white on black cars. The hood was known as the "Stinger" hood and is perhaps the most revered of any hood in Corvette history.

Jake and Elwood approved of the last C2 design. The biggest difference in appearance of the 1967's body was in the area behind the front wheels. The three vertical slots that were used on the '65 and '66 were replaced with a new design.

The new design was a single opening separated into five openings by four fins. It also tilted to the rear, giving it a much more aggressive appearance. From one angle it appeared solid, but from another the open areas were visible.

Another change took place on the rear of the car. The factory finally introduced a new backup light system. From 1963 to 1965, backup lights were an optional item. In 1966 they became a standard item. Either way, the lights resided in the innermost taillight position. In 1967 the backup lights were moved to the rear-center of the car in a stand alone position allowing both taillight lenses to be used for brake lights, running lights, and turn signals. Haz-

Few have mastered all Corvette facts. To properly restore a car, thousands of details must be known and adhered to. For instance, applying a straight edge to this 427 badge on this original car, it shows that the top of the 7 is lower than the 4 and 2. This is the proper factory positioning of the numbers.

One new body piece for 1967 was the big-block hood, which was installed on all cars with a 427-ci engine. Known as the "Stinger" hood, the piece is considered to be the greatest of the C2 hoods.

The big-block hood was actually a modified base hood with the scoop added. The scoop on the big-block hood was not functional and actually added drag, but it was worth it visually. It was a perfect visual reminder, or warning, that something nasty was under the hood.

The rear panel featured significant change as a new back-up light was introduced. Previous C2 back-up lights were all mounted in the innermost circular light fixtures, eliminating half of the brake lights. Some did not care for the new back-up light's fixture or positioning, which was high and in the center of the graceful rear panel. But the system scored high marks for functionality and safety.

The gas cap changed again in 1967. The new design still featured the crossed flags as the centerpiece, but they were now suspended on a circular field color matched to the car's body. The door framing and hinge were still finished in chrome.

Body Options

The scarce few options related to the body carried over from 1966. The A01 and A02 Soft Ray Glass options were both still available to lessen the sun's glare. The C07 Auxiliary Hardtop was still available to those who purchased convertibles, and 6,880 of the 14,436 sold were shipped with one of the $231 tops. The only new option related to the body had to do with the convertibles' optional hardtop. In 1967 the C08 Vinyl Covering for the C07 Auxiliary Hardtop was introduced. The option cost $52 and was added to 1,966 of the 6,880 tops shipped.

Interior

ard lights would become standard in 1967, meaning that the V74 option code used in 1966 to fit the car with hazard lights was dropped.

There were 10 exterior color choices available in 1967. Buyers could choose between Tuxedo Black, Ermine White, Rally Red, Marina Blue, Lynndale Blue, Elkhart Blue, Goodwood Green, Sunfire Yellow, Silver Pearl, and Marlboro Maroon. This meant that

Mosport Green and Milano Maroon, available in 1966, were dropped and that Goodwood Green and Marlboro Maroon took their place. Surprisingly, Goodwood Green was the most popular color in 1967, with 4,293 being so painted. Also a surprise was the fact that Tuxedo Black was again the least common color, with only 815 Tuxedo Black cars being produced.

With few exceptions, the 1967 interior was much like the 1966. With the new Corvette only a year away there was no point in making many changes. The interior still had molded carpet with vinyl

The new interior that engineers had on the drawing board would have to wait until 1968, so the beautiful C2 interior had one more run.

The main dash elements were the same in all C2s. It is interesting to note that as automakers move current models toward the retro look this 40-year-old design can stand with any of them. The knobs were changed in '67. They had the black center like the '66 but were a bit larger and more rounded.

The top dash of the '67 still housed the radio speaker and looked like the previous model, but there was a difference. Passengers lost their hold when the cutout on the passenger's side dash top was discontinued. The dash in the '67 was solid, unlike those of the previous four years.

With the exception of the new control knobs, the center dash stayed the same. This one is about as busy as they come, with air conditioning control and vent and an AM-FM radio.

The true teak steering wheel option was discontinued, so it was back to the plastic woodgrained wheel. The wheel was certainly adequate, but paled in comparison to the now extinct optional wheels.

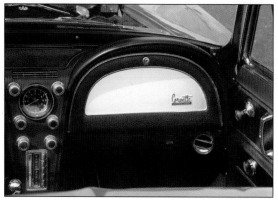

The glove box was always a handy element of the C2's interior. It gave driver and passenger a relatively large storage compartment that was easily accessible and lockable. It was one item that was sorely missed when the C3 debuted in 1968.

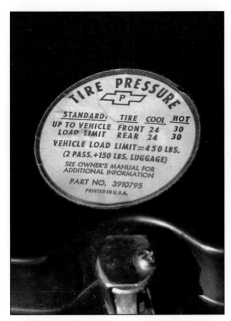

A sticker with the recommended tire pressures and the car's weight limits was located on the glove box door's inner surface.

A housing that was color matched to the interior covered the lever mechanism. The lever slot was sealed with a sliding shield. This design was used in 1967 and throughout C3 production. The brushed metal seatbelt buckles introduced in 1966 were used again in 1967.

The color-coded shifter plate was still around and was a design that changed little over the years, but behind it was a new feature. The emergency brake pull lever located under the dash was dropped with the introduction of the new lever between the seats. The C3 was to have this new emergency brake lever position; this item made it to production for 1967.

The seat covers were new for 1967, meaning that every year C2 had a different seat cover. Most cars came with vinyl seats—only 1,601 buyers chose the $79 leather seat covers. For the first time in the C2's history the seat back was locked into position. A small chrome lever was added to the seat back to release the lock so that the seat back could be tilted forward.

trimming around the edges. The seats had side-to-side stitching dividing the seal bottom and backrest into a large panel supported by smaller horizontal panels. The backrest of the seat locked for the first time in a C2.

In order to tilt the seat forward, a small chrome latch at the base of the seat's back panel had to be lifted.

The door panels also changed a bit when the door lock switch was moved forward, closer to the door handle. Many of the interior color choices were carried over from 1966. Black, red, Bright Blue, and Saddle all survived and were available in both vinyl and leather.

Green and two-tone white and blue were still available in vinyl only. The blue interior listed in 1966 was dropped and Teal Blue was added. This color was also available in either vinyl or leather. The silver interior, which was available in 1965 and 1966, was

The rear window was trimmed with color-matched pieces and retained with bright screws. The interior light was mounted forward of the window and had a white lens with a chrome base.

The little GM tag on the door actually adds a bit of safety as it is made from a very reflective material. If the door is opened on the side of the road at night it will be picked up in the headlights of cars coming from behind.

The '67 had retractable lap belts and optional shoulder belts. Only 1,426 cars were shipped with the $26 shoulder belts. Like many other parts of the car, each lap belt has a tag that is dated.

Molded nylon loop carpet covered the floor and rear of the coupe with all visible edges trimmed in vinyl. The rear of the coupe offered a fair amount of luggage space for a two-seater. The cover for the storage compartments had the carpet glued on with a chrome pull ring.

The door panels on the '67 were unique to the model year. The main difference was the repositioning of the door lock, which was moved forward from its position in '66 and was much easier to reach while seated in the car.

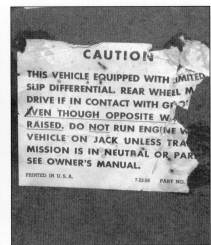

The rear compartments housed the jack and allowed space for a decent collection of tools. The jacking instructions were glued to the underside of the compartment door. On cars equipped with a Positraction rear end, a sticker was added warning the owner not to run the car in gear while on jack stands.

dropped altogether. The other new addition to the 1967 interior lineup was a white and black two-tone which was available in vinyl only.

INTERIOR OPTIONS

When outfitting the interior, the choices were almost all carried over from the 1966 production run. The tinted windows were still available under codes A01 and A02. Power windows, still coded A31, were added to just over 4,000 of the 1967s produced. The Telescoping Steering Column was added to 2,415 1967s, and was a bit different from its predecessors. The locking ring was changed, with the 1967 having only one more pronounced locking tab. The A82 Headrests and the A85 Shoulder Belt options both

returned after their 1966 introduction. The number of shoulder-belt-equipped cars grew from 37 in 1966 to 1,426 in 1967. The headrest became a bit smaller for 1967. Headrests were all vinyl,

even those added to leather seats.

The $412 C60 Air Conditioning was added to 3,788 Corvettes in 1967—the most ever. Leather seats were still priced at $79, but only 1,601 buyers,

The telescoping wheel was introduced in the 1965 model year and continued through the 1967 model. The system's locking ring was changed in 1967 with the new one having one large tab in place of the six small tabs on the locking ring used on the 1965 and 1966 models. The new ring was not as aesthetically pleasing as the old ring but did provide better leverage when locking the column.

In 1967 3,788 Corvettes were equipped with air conditioning. Changes to the interior included the vent and additional control knobs above the clock and the ducting with additional vents under the dash.

The 427 lineup was expanded in 1967. The horsepower dreams seemed limitless powered by high compression, cheap gas, and multiple carburetors. In 1967 small-block cars were still more common than big-block cars—but not by much. In 1967, 13,217 of the 22,940 Corvettes produced were shipped with a small-block. Only 6,858 shipped with the 300-hp base engine.

about 7 percent, opted for the high-grade seat covers. Once again, the highest volume optional item for the interior was the U69 AM-FM Radio. The price was still high ($172) yet the radio was added to 22,193 of the 22,940 1967 Corvettes produced. Buyers could still delete the heater and defroster systems and receive a $97 credit. The only new option affecting the interior was the U15 Speed Warning Indicator. When the U15 option was ordered the speedometer and tachometer had convex plastic lenses in place of the standard glass lenses. The option was only $10 and was installed on 2,108 1967s. The only interior option available in 1966 and not in 1967 was the N32 Teakwood Rimmed Steering Wheel.

ENGINE & DRIVETRAIN

Corvette buyers and C2 enthusiasts see 1967 as "the happy time" for powering a Corvette. In the C2's last year the total number of engines available was seven. The option list would contain six of them, offering buyers power—lots of power—probably too much power, and probably too much power with lightweight aluminum heads. And it was all done without fancy fuel injectors. It was done with compression, high fuel flow, and cubic

inches. Corvette buyers continued to make it worth Chevrolet's time to produce all of the optional engines. Of the 22,940 Corvettes produced in 1967, less than one in three had the base engine. At the end of the 1967 sales season 16,098 Corvettes had been produced with an optional engine.

The base engine for 1967 was still the 327-ci small-block. The engine was little changed with its 10.50:1 compression ratio and its four-barrel Holley carburetor. It kept the same power rating as 1966, still putting out 300 horsepower at 5,000 rpm and 360 ft-lbs of torque at 3,400 rpm. The engine featured a cast-iron manifold that was painted the same Chevrolet Orange as the engine. The base engine was the most popular single engine with 6,842 being produced in 1967, but it still represented less than 30 percent of production. If buyers elected to go to the option list for more horsepower,

The 350-hp L79 continued to be the most popular and thus the most common optional Corvette engine. Over one quarter of the '67s produced had the L79. It was a good compromise between power and streetability.

A properly installed fan shroud was essential to keep any C2 running cool, but especially the big-blocks. With the limited grille area of the car, efficient flow of air through the radiator was not the easiest design task. Small-block cars had a smaller radiator than those installed in big-blocks.

The L79 still came with a set of the finned aluminum valve covers and a set of "ram horn" manifolds. The spark plugs are shielded just below the manifold.

and most did, the only other small-block available was the L79. Also, the L79, like the base engine, had a 10.5:1 compression ratio and a four-barrel Holley carburetor. The engine was rated at 350 horsepower at 5,800 rpm and 360 ft-lbs of torque at 3,600 rpm. Unlike the base engine, the L79 sported an aluminum intake manifold left in its natural finish. The L79 was very popular in 1967, as many buyers wanted a bit more power without the weight, or expense, of a big-block. At year's end 6,375 L79s had been ordered, making it the second most popular engine and representing 27.8 percent of all production.

BIG-BLOCKS

The 427-ci engine had been mated to the Corvette in 1966 with two versions—the L36 and the L72. For 1967, the L72 code was discontinued but the L36 returned and was joined by three other big-block choices. The L36 was the entry-level 427 fueled with a four-barrel Holley carburetor mounted on a cast-iron manifold. The manifold was painted the same Chevrolet Orange as the engine.

Atop the engine was the traditional open-air performance air filter and housing with its chrome top and performance stickers. With 11.0:1

compression, the engine was rated at 390 horsepower at 5,400 rpm and a staggering 460 ft-lbs of torque at 3,600 rpm. The L36 was the most popular choice for big-block buyers. The cost was $200, which was not excessive for the amount of power returned. By year's end, 3,832 L36s had been installed at the factory.

The next step up on the big-block ladder was the L68. The main difference between this and the L36 was the fuel system. The engine was also a 427 with the same bore, stroke, and compression as the L36. In place of the single four-barrel carburetor found on the L36, the L68 was equipped with three

Nineteen sixty-seven was the second year that the 427 was available, and there were more versions of the monstrous engine to choose from. The L36 was the introductory level 427, costing $200. It provided the owner with an engine rated at 390 horsepower.

While the L36 had 40 more horsepower than the 350 horsepower of the hottest small-block motor, it did add a couple of hundred pounds. As a result the cars were quite similar in acceleration and the small-block car actually handled a bit better.

The ignition shielding on the big-block was a bit different from that on small-blocks. The cover over the distributor had a different shape and a bulge in the top. The shielding that ran down to the plugs was scrapped on the big-block and plug wires with a braided sheath were used.

The next step up on the 427 menu was a new motor—the L68. The engine set buyers back $305 and was rated at 400 horsepower with 460 ft-lbs of torque. In 1967, 2,101 cars were produced with L68s.

two-barrel carburetors. This system, known as the tripower, or three deuces, could be a bit more finicky than the single four-barrel and was only rated at 10 more horsepower. The L68 was rated at 400 horsepower at 5,400 rpm and 460 ft-lbs of torque at 3,600 rpm. At $305 the L68 was $105 more than the L36, which was pretty steep for the few

additional horsepower. Still, 2,101 buyers chose the L68 in 1967. The L68 was an attractive engine topped with the unique triangular air cleaner.

The third choice in big-blocks for 1967 was the L71. Another 427, the L71 shared the 11.0:1 with the L36 and L68; however, by using mechanical lifters and a more aggressive camshaft,

the engine produced even more horsepower. Like the L68, the L71 was fed with three two-barrel carburetors mounted on an aluminum manifold. The factory rated the engine at 435 horsepower at 5,800 rpm and 460 ft-lbs of torque at 4,000 rpm. While the L71 was about $130 more expensive than the L68, it produced significantly more

Like the L68, the L71 relied on three Holley carburetors to fuel the car.

On the L68, a three-deuce setup replaced the single four-barrel carburetor setup used on the other small- and big-block engines. The L68's fueling system relied on three two-barrel Holley carburetors on a special aluminum intake manifold. The carburetors were topped by a unique triangle-shaped air cleaner.

(35) horsepower and buyers once again proved that horsepower was what they wanted. In 1967, 3,754 Corvettes left St. Louis with an L71.

The top of the big-block food chain was the L88. The L88 was basically a race engine available in the 1967 Corvette. The price was high—an L88 added close to $1,000 to the price of a 1967 Corvette. The L88 was a 427 like the L36 and L71, but in place of the cast-iron cylinder heads the L88 was built using very efficient aluminum cylinder heads. The bore and stroke was the same as the other 427s; however, compression was wrenched up to 12.5:1. As a result, no other Corvette sounds quite like one equipped with an L88. A single 850-cfm Holley carburetor mounted on a special aluminum intake manifold fed the L88. It used mechanical lifters and a performance camshaft with heavy-duty valvetrain components. How much power the L88 actually produced is a somewhat cloudy issue. When it was released the engine did not have an official rating. The factory later rated the engine at 430 horsepower at 6,000 rpm, but most agreed that this was a very low estimate. Most felt that a more accurate rating was at least in the 500-hp range. The 20 1967 Corvettes with the L88 option have become legendary and are the holy grail of Corvette collecting.

The most powerful big-block in 1967 was the L71, which was also a new offering in the Corvette. The L71 was rated at 435 horsepower with 460 ft-lbs of torque. With 3,754 L71s being sold it meant that over 16 percent of the '67s had one of these incredible $437 power plants.

The last "L" code on the option list in 1967 was the L89. While it was an L code, the L89 was not an engine but actually a cylinder head option. When the L89 was ordered, buyers received an L71 with aluminum cylinder heads. Buyers paid $369 for the L89 option in addition to the $437 for the L71. The engine retained its 11.0:1 compression ratio and other than the heads it was just like the L71. With the L89 option the buyer could gain the weight-saving performance of the aluminum heads in an engine that was more streetable than the L88. Even so, only 16 people paid the additional fee for the aluminum heads in 1967, making L89 cars even more rare than the L88 cars.

Engine Options

The K66 Transistor Ignition System was installed on 5,759 engines in 1967, down from over 7,000 in 1966.

This is the underside of the mammoth 427. The engine was cradled low in the chassis with extra beefy motor mounts. This car was equipped with the optional side pipes so that the exhaust turned out instead of back. Note the heavy-duty starter needed to turn over the high-displacement engine.

When a car was equipped with side pipes the exhaust ran outward from the manifold instead of rearward. The profile of the heat shield is visible, as is its location relative to the actual exhaust pipe.

The N14 Side Mount Exhaust System option continued to rise in popularity and was installed on 4,209 1967s in place of the standard exhaust. The N11 Off-Road Exhaust System also remained on the option list. With a sales number of 2,326, it was added to over 10 percent of the 1967s produced. The K19 Air Injector Reactor was still required on cars sold in California and was added to 2,573 engines. The N03 36-Gallon Fuel Tank was also still on the option list. This option was available on every year of the C2, but in 1967 was only added to two cars.

DRIVETRAIN

Transmission choices in 1967 were identical to those in 1966. The standard three-speed manual unit was only installed in 424 Corvettes in 1967;

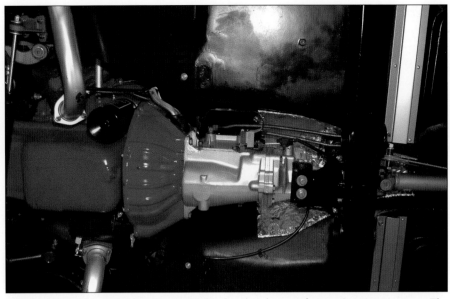

The four-speed transmission continued to be the choice of most Corvette owners. The shift linkage is attached on the left side of the transmission. Note the heat shield in the tunnel above the transmission. It was an effort to keep as much heat as possible out of the cockpit.

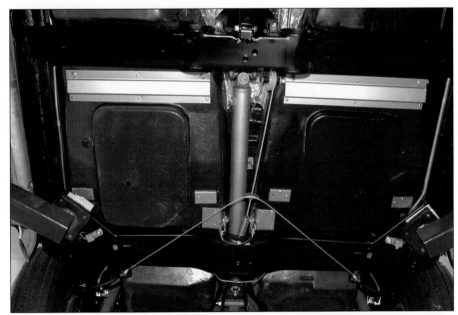

The driveshaft was plumbed through a crossmember on its way to the rear gear. It was hinged with "U" joints at both front and rear.

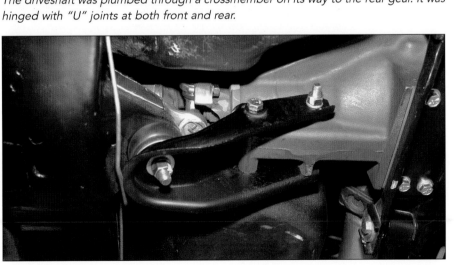

Rear gears were available in the Corvette with ratios ranging from a 3:08:1 highway gear to a stump-pulling 4.56:1. Throughout C2 production most cars were equipped with a Positraction rear gear. Cars so equipped had a tag on the fluid filler warning owners and mechanics to use the proper lubricant.

The rear gear was secured with a heavy-duty bracket bolted to the crossmember. The thick rubber bushing in the mount was used to dampen shock and vibration.

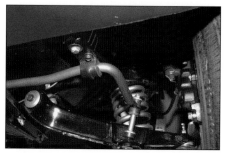

The front sway bar linked the front of the chassis to the front suspension. The bar was mounted to the chassis using brackets with thick rubber bushings. The ends of the bar connected to the lower control arms with very strong bolts that also had bushings.

On each side of the gear a half-shaft transferred the power to the wheel. When designing the Corvette, engineers had to put lots of stuff in a relatively small car. Note how the half shaft has very little clearance forward. This "tub" is the underside of the storage well for the jack just behind the passenger's seat.

Ball joints were riveted in at the factory, but few cars remained that way. When replaced, the rivets were chiseled away and the replacement ball joints were mounted with bolts.

meaning 92 percent of the cars had an optional gearbox. The most popular was the M21 close ratio four-speed. With 11,015 units being sold, almost half of the 1967s came with an M21. Close behind was the M20, which was installed in 9,157 cars. The price of both transmissions was $184. People who did not want to shift (2,324) chose the trusty old M35 Powerglide. Like 1966, the least common transmission was the M22 heavy-duty unit. Surprisingly, only 20 of "the rock crusher" $237 transmissions were sold.

In the rear the G82 Positraction option was installed on 20,308, about 89 percent of the cars produced. Once again, buyers could choose between gears with ratios of 3.08:1, 3.36:1, 3.55:1, 3.70:1, 4.11:1, or 4.56:1.

SUSPENSION, STEERING & BRAKES

The suspension and steering systems did not change from 1966. The N40 Power Steering option was added to 5,747 Corvettes in 1967. The F41 Special Front and Rear Suspension was also still available for a very reasonable $36. The suspension and steering remained the same for 1967; however, there was a significant change to the Corvette's brake system. Beginning in 1967 a Federal Law mandated that cars be produced with a dual-circuit hydraulic system. The stock brakes on previous Corvettes were all a single-circuit design. This meant a single piston was pushing fluid in a single line from the master cylinder. This single line was then split to the brakes on all four corners.

On a dual-circuit system there

The front suspension was essentially unchanged from the earliest C2. In fact, the same suspension, steering, and brake system would remain in use through the life of the C3. The car still made use of the front-end Impala parts that Duntov agreed to use to drop production costs. The lower control arms were finished in black and the shocks in grey. The shock's bottom mount is visible through the hole in the control arm.

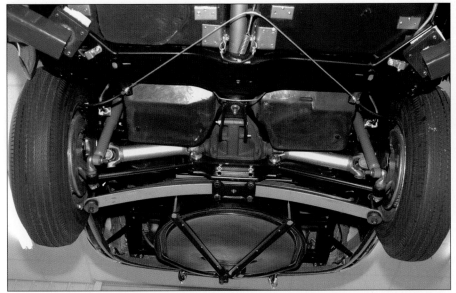

The leaf spring was attached directly under the gear with a lower plate and four very strong bolts.

Duntov's compromise on the front suspension was in order to get the rear suspension that he wanted. The independent rear suspension was added to the Corvette in 1963 and the car has had an independent rear ever since. The independent rear suspension was aligned differently from a solid axle car. The toe was set with shims at the front of the trailing arm. The camber was set using this radius rod. The bolt that connected the inner side of the rod to the gear had a cam-type washer that positioned the bar inwards or outwards, thus changing the angle of the wheel assembly. The new parking brake cable ran from the lever between the seats to this point where it was attached to a second cable that ran to each rear wheel.

Due to federal regulations a dual-circuit master cylinder was added to the Corvette. This system had two separate lines exiting the unit—one for the front and one for the rear. If one were severed the other still provided pressure to stop the car.

The rear of the trailing arm was a busy area on the Corvette. The leaf spring was connected with strong bolts that were cushioned with rubber bushings. The half-shaft, with its "U" joint, passed through the trailing arm just forward of the spring. Below it, a radius rod was used to square the rear end and adjust the camber. This big-block car also has a sway bar that is attached to the trailing arm at the top.

Other than the master cylinder, the disc brake system introduced in 1965 remained unchanged. In fact, the Corvette's brakes remained pretty much unchanged until the end of C3 production in 1982.

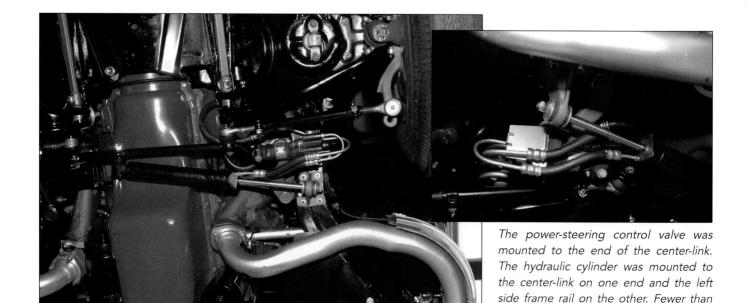

The power-steering control valve was mounted to the end of the center-link. The hydraulic cylinder was mounted to the center-link on one end and the left side frame rail on the other. Fewer than 6,000 cars were equipped with power steering in 1967. When so equipped, the system's pump was mounted on the left side of the engine below the alternator.

The optional aluminum wheels also changed in 1967. The knock-offs were gone, a victim of safety concerns. The wheel available in 1967 had the same overall design as the knock-offs, but was attached with the standard five lug nuts, which were hidden under the new center cap.

were two lines being supplied by a dual piston in the master cylinder. One line supplied the front brakes and one supplied the rear brakes. The dual-circuit system was safer because if one line was damaged and ceased to function, the other line still worked and allowed for some braking ability. Dual-circuit brakes were not new to the Corvette program. Back in 1963 the Z06 option added dual-cylinder technology to the Z06's drum brakes.

The stock brakes were supported by two options. The $42 J50 Power Brakes were added to 4,766 1967s, which was about 21 percent. The J56

Special Heavy Duty Brakes—resurrected for 1966—were also still available, but still priced at a staggering $342. Only the most dutiful performance enthusiast chose them, as only 267 cars were equipped with the option.

There were significant changes in the area of wheels for the 1967 year. The standard Corvette wheel was finally changed. The wheel was still a steel unit with a 15-inch diameter; however, the width grew to 5 inches. The wheel was also styled differently, with five rectangular slots around its midsection. Wheel covers had

changed often during the Corvette's production and in 1967 the base wheel came with yet another new covering. This time the factory got it right and the new design would last for many a year. The one-piece wheel cover design used from 1963 to 1966 was discontinued. For 1967 the standard steel wheel was accented with a chrome-trim ring on the outside edge of the wheel and a small center cap that covered the hubs and lug nuts. The center cap was inscribed with "Chevrolet Motor Division," as well as the words "Disc Brakes." Thus the rally wheel began its long, popular run

The steel wheel with full-sized hubcap arrangement used from 1963 to 1966 was dropped and the Rally Wheel combination made its first appearance. The setup featured a painted rim with a chrome outer trim ring and a separate center cap. This design was wildly popular on many Chevrolet models and became a muscle car classic.

on Corvettes. Although the center cap changed over the years, the rally wheel package was around for many years on various Chevrolet cars.

The optional wheels also changed in 1967. Lightweight aluminum wheels were still available from the option list under the code N89 and were dropped in price to $263. However, the wheels themselves were quite different as the knock-off system was discontinued. Chevrolet was under pressure to get rid of knock-offs due to safety concerns. As a result, 1966 was the last year a true knock-off was available. For 1967, the optional wheels kept the same general appearance, but were secured with the traditional five-lug with a camouflaged center cap.

The standard tire was still a 7.75 x 15 rayon blackwall. The P92 option continued to be the most popular choice, with 13,445 sets being sold. The T01 Goldwall Tires option was offered preproduction, but was discontinued before the cars were built and disappeared from the option list altogether. A new tire took its place—the nylon QB1 Redline Tire, which was quite popular, with 4,230 being sold. The tire was so popular that

over the years many Corvettes shipped from the factory with white-walls were changed to Redlines. Goodyear, Firestone, B.F. Goodrich, General, and U.S. Royal continued to be the Corvette tire suppliers.

1967 Summary

In 1967 sales of the Corvette were down. In 1966 the Corvette team had almost achieved their long-time goal of 30,000 units, clocking in at 27,720. But in 1967 sales dropped over 17 percent, with the total sales figure topping out at 22,940 cars. This was split between 8,504 coupes and 14,436 convertibles. The total revenue produced was $37,315,552 in coupes, $61,208,640 in convertibles, and $19,535,518 in option revenue, for a grand total of $118,059,710.

C2 Curtain Call

As we look back at the years of the C2, its lifespan seems so short. In the five years of C2 production 117,964 cars were produced. Those that remain are some of the most classic antique cars ever produced. Currently, any pristine C2 with significant options can

easily fetch over $100,000, and the pricing of the very rare cars seems limitless. Throughout its life the car had styling and engineering that ranged from adequate to cutting-edge. The power options ranged from the better-than-adequate 250-hp base engine of 1963 to the incredible 400-plus horsepower big-blocks of 1965, '66, and '67. A C2 could be purchased with air conditioning, a mild V-8 and automatic transmission for the wife, or a stripped-down 435-hp, four-speed performance machine. But it was the latter that kept the Corvette alive. Higher-priced optional engines were almost always put in Corvettes, and automatic transmissions were few. The C2 was the great transition in Corvette history. The team of performance enthusiasts that designed the car took the Corvette image and reputation to a new plateau. Thoughts of C1s are full of images of girls with bows in their hair and guys with white slacks and buck shoes at picnics. Thoughts of the C2 contain images of a grinning maniac romping on a 1967 with a 427—and lots of smoke. The C2 was the Corvette where performance became the standard. It was a rare occasion where the performance attitude of the engineers was matched by the imagination of the stylists.

The C3 took the Corvette baton in 1968. Some liked the new body and some did not. Some liked the new interior and some did not. For a while the engine power grew, until the fun ended in the early 1970s and performance went south—way south. In 1970 the power game peaked with the 465-hp 454s. By 1975 the most powerful optional engine was the L82 350 with a 205-hp rating. Even with its different bodies, interiors, and engines, the chassis, suspension, brakes, and drivetrain were all pretty much the same as the C2. When perusing the Corvette catalogs it is common to see many of these parts for cars ranging from mid 1963 to 1982 when C3 production ended. Its legacy did not truly end until 1984, when the C4 cut all of the ties from the glory years of the 1963 to 1967 Corvettes.

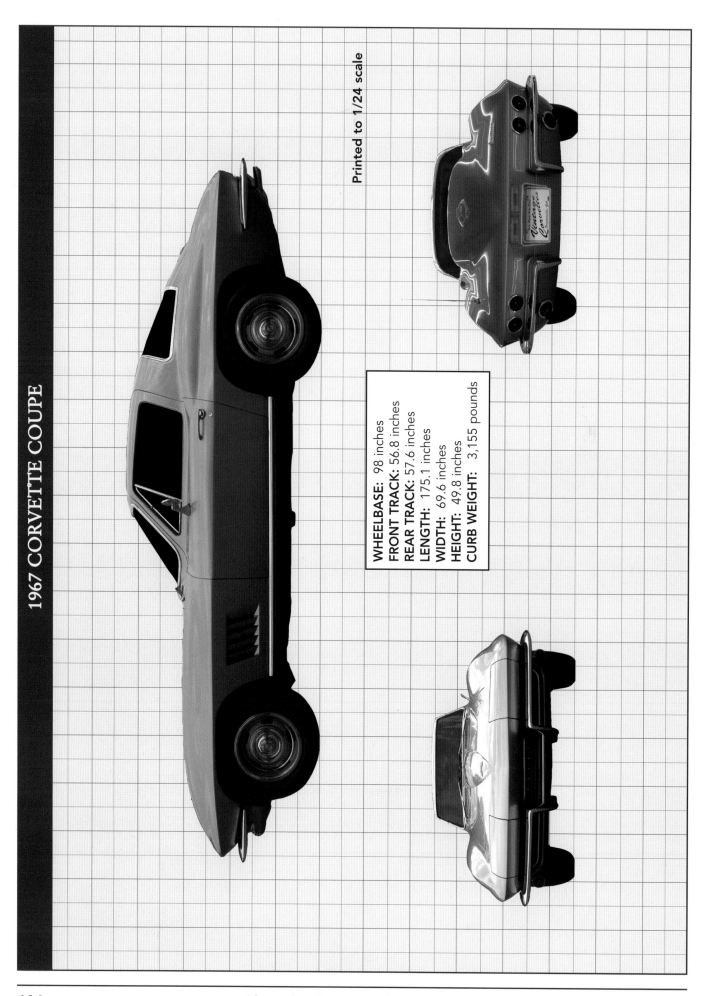

1967 CORVETTE COUPE

Printed to 1/24 scale

WHEELBASE: 98 inches
FRONT TRACK: 56.8 inches
REAR TRACK: 57.6 inches
LENGTH: 175.1 inches
WIDTH: 69.6 inches
HEIGHT: 49.8 inches
CURB WEIGHT: 3,155 pounds

1967 CORVETTE CONVERTIBLE

Printed to 1/24 scale

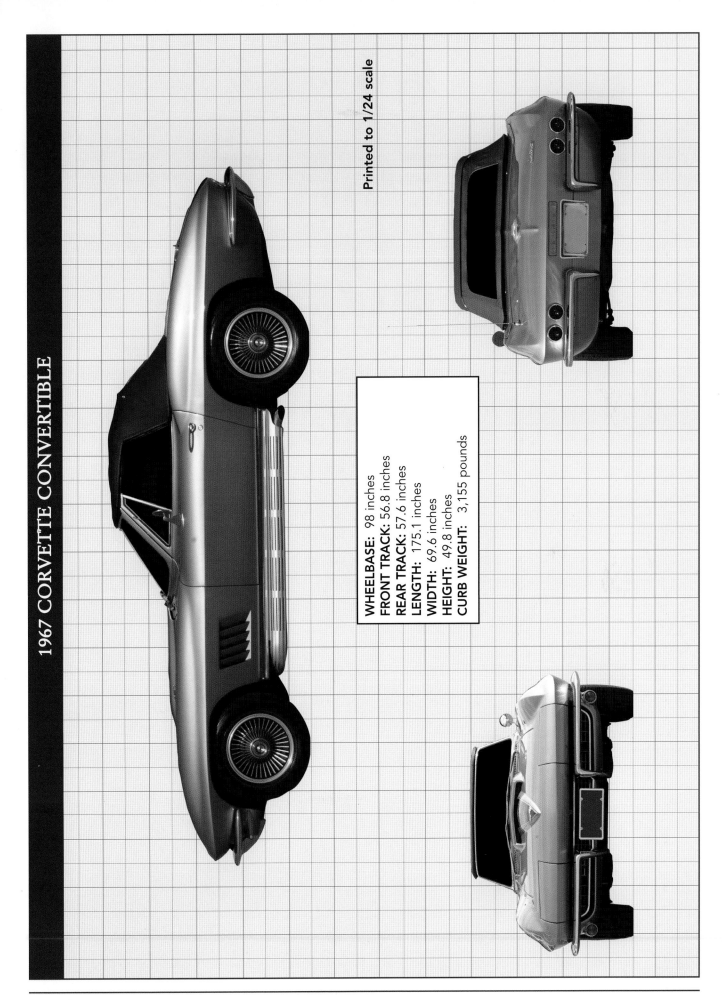

WHEELBASE: 98 inches
FRONT TRACK: 56.8 inches
REAR TRACK: 57.6 inches
LENGTH: 175.1 inches
WIDTH: 69.6 inches
HEIGHT: 49.8 inches
CURB WEIGHT: 3,155 pounds

6

MODELING the 1963 to 1967 CORVETTE

BY PAT COVERT

Corvette models have always been a favorite of car modelers, but none capture the minds—and wallets—of kit builders as much as the beloved second-generation Sting Rays of 1963–1967. So much so that these model kits from the years have rarely been out of re-issue and two major model car manufacturers continue to re-issue and put out newer versions of this captivating car today. The first manufacturer to produce a kit of the 1963 Corvette was juggernaut manufacturer AMT, who would produce annual kits of the sports car each year through 1967 in the standard 1/25 scale. Every other major kit manufacturer has produced a version of the second generation since, including Revell and Monogram, who have since merged, and MPC, who was bought up by AMT. In addition to bone stock models there have been many versions of Corvette concept cars, street machines, and racecars released over the past four decades.

First-issue annual kits of the AMT 1963–'67 Corvettes have become high-dollar collectibles, but model builders

need not despair; AMT has put out ample re-releases since of their 1963 coupe and convertible that can be had for prices not much higher than you'd pay for a current release. As was the norm back in 1963, the AMT kit included stock, custom and drag

options so these kits are loaded with extras. Options include a choice of a 327 or 427 engines and each of these can be built stock or goosed up with hot rod parts. This kit has held up extremely well over the years and the only drawbacks, once again typical of

Corvettes have always been popular among car modelers! Shown above is the Revell-Monogram '67 427 convertible skillfully built by modeler Tim Kolankiewitz.

The AMT 1963 Corvette coupe is an older kit, but it has stood up well over the years and has been re-released many times so it is easy to find—and affordable.

Here's the Monogram version (released under both the Revell and Monogram brand names) of the 1967 427 convertible, a great kit for building straight out of the box or super-detailing.

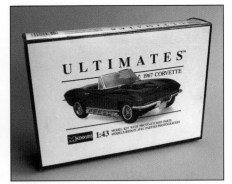

The Monogram Ultimates 1/43rd scale '67 Corvette packs loads of detail for its small size. If you don't mind working small, this is a kit that builds up into a fantastic replica.

the day, to the model are the steel axles which take the place of full suspension detail and the bucket seats are molded into the interior assembly. Get past these two peccadilloes and you can build a very nice version of the car.

Those desiring a 1/25 scale 1967 Corvette suited for building an accurate shelf model or super-detailed contest winner need look no farther than the Revell-Monogram kit. This is a relatively new tooling (1995) with a full array of suspension components, engine details, and interior parts. This kit, available in coupe and convertible configurations, has only been offered with the 427 engine option, but it would easy to do a 327 conversion given the many Chevy kits available for kit-bashing. Hood decals in white, black, bright blue and red allow the builder to replicate any color version Corvette available for the year and super-detailers can pick up photo-etched aftermarket details, which include realistic details such as a more precise grill and scripts, for the ultimate in accuracy. The aftermarket also offers conversion parts for back-dating the 1967 Corvette to previous years. This kit is a bonanza for second-generation Corvette lovers and is a mainstay in the Revell-Monogram line so it is both easy to find and affordable.

One of the most detailed Corvette models ever offered is the Monogram 1/43 scale 1967 Corvette Ultimates kit. This is a small scale model that is huge when it comes to detailing options, replete with a 427 engine, detailed chassis and interior, hood accent striping, and even a set of photo-etched parts. If you can handle the challenges

AMT offered the 1963 Corvette in both a convertible and coupe, shown here side by side for comparison. Inside the box you'll find a host of custom and drag racing parts in addition to all the stock fare.

of small-scale modeling this kit builds up into a remarkable replica.

Racecar modelers will be delighted at the brand new release of the 1966 Penske Racing Corvette by Revell. This kit is done up in 1/24 scale and accurately reproduces the blue 427-powered Sunoco sponsored car that ran at Sebring. If you want to dig a lit-

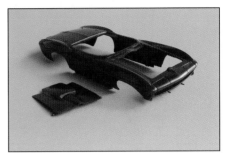

This is the out-of-the-box Revell-Monogram 1967 Corvette convertible body. A chrome windshield frame is separate from the body making for a highly accurate finished model.

tle deeper you can still find many of the old MPC second-generation Corvettes at model car shows and on Internet auction houses such as eBay. In fact, these are two great places to start in your quest for both new and old issue 1963-'67, so the sooner you get hopping the faster you can start building the scale Corvette of your dreams!

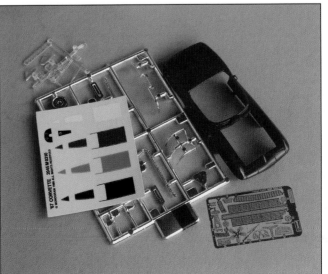

Shown here is just a sampling of what you'll find inside the Monogram 1/43 scale '67 Corvette. A detailed engine, chassis, and interior are also included. Note the tree of fine photo-etch detailing components in the lower right.

1963

RPO#	DESCRIPTION	Quantity	Price
837	Base Corvette Coupe	10,594	$4,257.00
867	Base Corvette Convertible	10,919	$4,037.00
898	Genuine Leather Seats	1,114	$80.70
941	Sebring Silver Paint	3,516	$80.70
A01	Soft Ray Tinted Glass (all windows)	629	$16.15
A02	Soft Ray Tinted Glass, (windshield only)	470	$10.80
A31	Power Windows	3,742	$59.20
C07	Auxiliary Hardtop (convertible)	5,739	$236.75
C48	Heater and Defroster Deletion (credit)	124	($100.00)
C60	Air Conditioning	278	$421.80
G81	Positraction Rear Axle - all ratios	17,554	$43.05
G91	Special Highway Axle - 3.08:1 ratio	211	$2.20
J50	Power Brakes	3,336	$43.05
J65	Sintered Metallic Brakes	5,310	$37.70
L75	327ci, 300 hp Engine	8,033	$53.80
L76	327ci, 340 hp Engine	6,978	$107.60
L84	327ci, 360 hp Engine	2,610	$430.40
M20	4-Speed Manual Transmission	17,973	$188.30
M35	Powerglide Automatic Transmission	2,621	$199.10
N03	36-Gallon Fuel Tank (coupe)	63	$202.30
N11	Off-Road Exhaust System		$37.70
N34	Woodgrained Plastic Steering Wheel	130	$16.15
N40	Power Steering	3,063	$75.35
P48	Cast Aluminum Knock-Off Wheels		$322.80
P91	Blackwall Tires, 6.70x15 (Nylon cord)	412	$15.70
P92	Whitewall Tires, 6.70x15 (Rayon cord)	19,383	$31.50
T86	Back-up Lamps	318	$10.80
U65	Signal Seeking AM Radio	11,368	$137.75
U69	AM-FM Radio	9,178	$174.35
Z06	Special Performance Equipment	199	$1,818.45

1964

RPO#	DESCRIPTION	Quantity	Price
837	Base Corvette Coupe	8,304	$4,252.00
867	Base Corvette Convertible	13,925	$4,037.00
	Genuine Leather Seats	1,334	$80.70
A01	Soft Ray Tinted Glass, (all windows)	6,031	$16.15
A02	Soft Ray Tinted Glass, (windshield only)	6,387	$10.80
A31	Power Windows	3,706	$59.20
C07	Auxiliary Hardtop (convertible)	7,023	$236.75
C48	Heater and Defroster Deletion (credit)	60	($100.00)
C60	Air Conditioning	1,988	$421.80
F40	Special Front and Rear Suspension	82	$37.70
G81	Positraction Rear Axle - all ratios	18,279	$43.05
G91	Special Highway Axle - 3.08:1 ratio	2,310	$2.20
J50	Power Brakes	2,270	$43.05
J56	Special Sintered Metallic Brakes	29	$629.00
J65	Sintered Metallic Brakes, (powered)	4,780	$53.80
K66	Transistor Ignition System	552	$75.35
L75	327ci, 300 hp Engine	10,471	$53.80
L76	327ci, 365 hp Engine	7,171	$107.60
L84	327ci, 375 hp Engine	1,325	$538.00
M20	4-Speed Manual Transmission	19,034	$188.30
M35	Powerglide Automatic Transmission	2,480	$199.10
N03	36-Gallon Fuel Tank (coupe)	38	$202.30
N11	Off-Road Exhaust System	1,953	$37.70
N40	Power Steering	3,126	$75.35
P48	Cast Aluminum Knock-Off Wheels	806	$322.80
P91	Blackwall Tires, 6.70x15 (Nylon cord)	372	$15.70
P92	Whitewall Tires, 6.70x15 (Rayon cord)	19,977	$31.85
T86	Back-up Lamps	11,085	$10.80
U69	AM-FM Radio	20,934	$176.50

1965

RPO#	DESCRIPTION	Quantity	Price
19437	Base Corvette Coupe	8,186	$4,321.00
19467	Base Corvette Convertible	15,376	$4,106.00
	Genuine Leather Seats	2,128	$80.70
A01	Soft Ray Tinted Glass, (all windows)	8,752	$16.15
A02	Soft Ray Tinted Glass, (windshield only)	7,624	$10.80
A31	Power Windows	3,809	$59.20
C07	Auxiliary Hardtop (convertible)	7,787	$236.75
C48	Heater and Defroster Deletion (credit)	39	($100.00)
C60	Air Conditioning	2,423	$421.80
F40	Special Front and Rear Suspension	975	$37.70
G81	Positraction Rear Axle - all ratios	19,965	$43.05
G91	Special Highway Axle - 3.08:1 ratio	1,886	$2.20
J50	Power Brakes	4,044	$43.05
J61	Drum Brakes (substitution credit)	316	($64.50)
K66	Transistor Ignition System	3,686	$75.35
L75	327ci, 300 hp Engine	8,358	$53.80
L76	327ci, 365 hp Engine	5,011	$129.15
L78	396ci, 425 hp Engine	2,157	$292.70
L79	327ci, 350 hp Engine	4,716	$107.60
L84	327ci, 375 hp Engine	771	$538.00
M20	4-Speed Manual Transmission	21,107	$188.30
M35	Powerglide Automatic Transmission	2,021	$199.10
N03	36-Gallon Fuel Tank (coupe)	41	$202.30
N11	Off-Road Exhaust System	2,468	$37.70
N14	Side Mount Exhaust System	759	$134.50
N32	Teakwood Steering Wheel	2,259	$48.45
N36	Telescopic Steering Column	3,917	$43.05
N40	Power Steering	3,236	$96.85
P48	Cast Aluminum Knock-Off Wheels	1,116	$322.80
P91	Blackwall Tires, 7.75x15 (nylon cord)	168	$15.70
P92	Whitewall Tires, 7.75x15 (rayon cord)	19,300	$31.85
T01	Goldwall Tires, 7.75x15 (nylon cord)	989	$50.05
U69	AM-FM Radio	22,113	$203.40
Z01	Comfort and Convenience Group	15,397	$16.15

1966

RPO#	DESCRIPTION	Quantity	Price
19437	Base Corvette Coupe	9,958	$4,295.00
19467	Base Corvette Convertible	17,762	$4,084.00
	Genuine Leather Seats	2,002	$79.00
A01	Soft Ray Tinted Glass, all windows	11,859	$15.80
A02	Soft Ray Tinted Glass, windshield	9,270	$10.55
A31	Power Windows	4,562	$57.95
A82	Headrests	1,033	$42.15
A85	Shoulder Belts	37	$26.35
C07	Auxiliary Hardtop (convertible)	8,463	$231.75
C48	Heater and Defroster Deletion (credit)	54	($97.85)
C60	Air Conditioning	3,520	$412.90
F41	Special Front and Rear Suspension	2,705	$36.90
G81	Positraction Rear Axle - all ratios	24,056	$42.15
J50	Power Brakes	5,464	$42.15
J56	Special Heavy Duty Brakes	382	$342.30
K19	Air Injection Reactor	2,380	$44.75
K66	Transistor Ignition System	7,146	$73.75
L36	427ci, 390 hp Engine	5,116	$181.20
L72	427ci, 450/425 hp Engine	5,258	$312.85
L79	327ci, 350 hp Engine	7,591	$105.35
M20	4-Speed Manual Transmission	10,837	$184.35
M21	4-Speed Man Trans, close ratio	13,903	$184.35
M22	4-Speed Man Trans, close ratio, HD	15	$237.00
M35	Powerglide Automatic Transmission	2,401	$194.85
N03	36-Gallon Fuel Tank (coupe)	66	$198.05
N11	Off-Road Exhaust System	2,795	$36.90
N14	Side Mount Exhaust System	3,617	$131.65
N32	Teakwood Steering Wheel	3,941	$47.40
N36	Telescopic Steering Column	3,670	$42.15
N40	Power Steering	5,611	$94.80
P48	Cast Aluminum Knock-Off Wheels	1,194	$316.00
P92	Whitewall Tires, 7.75x15 (rayon cord)	17,969	$31.30
T01	Goldwall Tires, 7.75x15 (nylon cord)	5,557	$46.55
U69	AM-FM Radio	26,363	$199.10
V74	Traffic Hazard Lamp Switch	5,764	$11.60

1967

RPO#	DESCRIPTION	Quantity	Price
19437	Base Corvette Coupe	8,504	$4,388.75
19467	Base Corvette Convertible	14,436	$4,240.75
	Genuine Leather Seats	1,601	$79.00
A01	Soft Ray Tinted Glass, all windows	11,331	$15.80
A02	Soft Ray Tinted Glass, windshield	6,558	$10.55
A31	Power Windows	4,036	$57.95
A82	Headrests	1,762	$42.15
A85	Shoulder Belts	1,426	$26.35
C07	Auxiliary Hardtop (convertible)	6,880	$231.75
C08	Vinyl Covering (for auxiliary hardtop)	1,966	$52.70
C48	Heater and Defroster Deletion (credit)	35	($97.85)
C60	Air Conditioning	3,788	$412.90
F41	Special Front and Rear Suspension	2,198	$36.90
G81	Positraction Rear Axle - all ratios	20,308	$42.15
J50	Power Brakes	4,766	$42.15
J56	Special Heavy Duty Brakes	267	$342.30
K19	Air Injection Reactor	2,573	$44.75
K66	Transistor Ignition System	5,759	$73.75
L36	427ci, 390 hp Engine	3,832	$200.15
L68	427ci, 400 hp Engine	2,101	$305.50
L71	427ci, 435 hp Engine	3,754	$437.10
L79	327ci, 350 hp Engine	6,375	$105.35
L82	427ci, 430 hp Engine	20	$947.90
L89	Aluminum Cylinder Heads for L71	16	$368.65
M20	4-Speed Manual Transmission	9,157	$184.35
M21	4-Speed Man Trans, close ratio	11,015	$184.35
M22	4-Speed Man Trans, close ratio, HD	20	$237.00
M35	Powerglide Automatic Transmission	2,324	$194.85
N03	36-Gallon Fuel Tank (coupe)	2	$198.05
N11	Off-Road Exhaust System	2,326	$36.90
N14	Side Mount Exhaust System	4,209	$131.65
N36	Telescopic Steering Column	2,415	$42.15
N40	Power Steering	5,747	$94.80
N89	Cast Aluminum Wheels (bolt-on)	720	$263.30
P92	Whitewall Tires, 7.75x15	13,445	$31.35
QB1	Redline Tires, 7.75x15	4,230	$46.65
U15	Speed Warning Indicator	2,108	$10.55
U69	AM-FM Radio	22,193	$172.75

Interior Colors

1963	1964	1965	1966	1967
Black Vinyl	Black Vinyl	Black Vinyl	Black Vinyl	Black Vinyl
Red Vinyl	Black Leather	Black Leather	Black Leather	Black Leather
Dark Blue Vinyl	Red Vinyl	Red Vinyl	Red Vinyl	Red Vinyl
Saddle Vinyl	Red Leather	Red Leather	Red Leather	Red Leather
Saddle Leather	Blue Vinyl	Blue Vinyl	Blue Vinyl	Saddle Vinyl
	Blue Leather	Blue Leather	Blue Leather	Saddle Leather
	Saddle Vinyl	Saddle Vinyl	Saddle Vinyl	Green Vinyl
	Saddle Leather	Saddle Leather	Saddle Leather	Bright Blue Vinyl
	Silver and Black Vinyl	Green Vinyl	Green Vinyl	Bright Blue Leather
	Silver and Black Leather	Green Leather	Silver Vinyl	Teal Blue Vinyl
	Silver and Blue Vinyl	Silver Vinyl	Silver Leather	Teal Blue Leather
	Silver and Blue Leather	Silver Leather	Bright Blue Vinyl	White and Blue Vinyl
	White and Black Vinyl	White and Red Leather	Bright Blue Leather	White and Black Vinyl
	White and Black Leather	White and Blue Vinyl	White and Blue Vinyl	
	White and Blue Vinyl	White and Blue Leather		
	White and Blue Leather			
	White and Red Vinyl			
	White and Red Leather			
	White and Saddle Vinyl			
	White and Saddle Leather			

Engine Popularity

1963

Code	Engine	Produced	Percent	Price
BASE	327 - 250 Horsepower	3,892	18.1%	
L75	327 - 300 Horsepower	8,033	37.3%	$53.00
L76	327 - 340 Horsepower	6,978	32.4%	$107.00
L84	327 - 360 Horsepower	2,610	12.1%	$430.00

1964

Code	Engine	Produced	Percent	Price
BASE	327 - 250 Horsepower	3,262	14.7%	
L75	327 - 300 Horsepower	10,471	47.1%	$53.00
L76	327 - 365 Horsepower	7,171	32.3%	$107.00
L84	327 - 375 Horsepower	1,325	6.0%	$538.00

1965

Code	Engine	Produced	Percent	Price
BASE	327 - 250 Horsepower	2,549	10.8%	
L75	327 - 300 Horsepower	8,358	35.5%	$53.00
L76	327 - 365 Horsepower	5,011	21.3%	$129.00
L78	396 - 425 Horsepower	2,157	9.2%	$292.00
L79	327 - 350 Horsepower	4,716	20.0%	$107.00
L84	327 - 375 Horsepower	771	3.3%	$538.00

1966

Code	Engine	Produced	Percent	Price
BASE	327 - 300 Horsepower	9,755	35.2%	
L36	427 - 390 Horsepower	5,116	18.5%	$181.00
L72	427 - 450 Horsepower	5,258	19.0%	$312.00
L79	327 - 350 Horsepower	7,591	27.4%	$105.00

1967

Code	Engine	Produced	Percent	Price
BASE	327 - 300 Horsepower	6,858	29.9%	
L36	427 - 390 Horsepower	3,832	16.7%	$200.00
L68	427 - 400 Horsepower	2,101	9.2%	$305.00
L71	427 - 435 Horsepower	3,754	16.4%	$437.00
L79	327 - 350 Horsepower	6,375	27.8%	$105.00
L88	427 - 430 Horsepower	20	0.09%	$947.00
L89	Aluminum Cylinder Heads w/L71	16	0.07%	$368.00

Engine Power Chart

1963	CI	HP	RPM	TORQ	RPM	BORE	STRK	1966	CI	HP	RPM	TORQ	RPM	BORE	STRK
BASE	327	250	4400	350	2800	4.00	3.25	BASE	327	300	5000	360	3200	4.00	3.25
L75	327	300	5000	360	3200	4.00	3.25	L79	327	350	5800	360	3600	4.00	3.25
L76	327	340	6000	344	4000	4.00	3.25	L36	427	390	5200	460	3600	4.00	4.125
L84	327	360	6000	352	4000	4.00	3.25	L72	427	425	5600	460	4000	4.00	4.125

1964	CI	HP	RPM	TORQ	RPM	BORE	STRK	1967	CI	HP	RPM	TORQ	RPM	BORE	STRK
BASE	327	250	4400	350	2800	4.00	3.25	BASE	327	300	5000	360	3400	4.00	3.25
L75	327	300	5000	360	3200	4.00	3.25	L79	327	350	5800	360	3600	4.00	3.25
L76	327	365	6200	350	4000	4.00	3.25	L36	427	390	5400	460	3600	4.00	4.125
L84	327	375	6200	350	4800	4.00	3.25	L68	427	400	5400	460	3600	4.00	4.125
								L71	427	435	5800	460	4000	4.00	4.125
1965	CI	HP	RPM	TORQ	RPM	BORE	STRK	L88	427	430	6000	352	4000	4.00	4.125
BASE	327	250	4400	350	2800	4.00	3.25	L89	427	435	6000	352	4000	4.00	4.125
L75	327	300	5000	360	3200	4.00	3.25								
L76	327	365	6200	344	4000	4.00	3.25								
L84	327	375	6200	350	4800	4.00	3.25								
L78	396	425	6400	352	4000	4.09	3.76								
L79	327	350	5800	360	3800	4.00	3.25								

Options by Popularity

1963

RPO#	Description	Quantity	Percent
P92	6.70x15 Whitewall Tires	19,383	90.1%
M20	4-Speed Manual Transmission	17,973	83.5%
G81	Positraction Rear Axle	17,554	81.6%
U85	Signal Seeking AM Radio	11,368	52.8%
U69	AM-FM Radio	9,178	42.7%
L75	327ci, 300 hp Engine	8,033	37.3%
L76	327ci, 340 hp Engine	6,978	32.4%
C07	Auxiliary Hardtop (convertible)	5,739	52.6%
J65	Sintered Metallic Brakes	5,310	24.7%
A31	Power Windows	3,742	17.4%
941	Sebring Silver Exterior Paint	3,516	16.3%
J50	Power Brakes	3,336	15.5%
N40	Power Steering	3,063	14.2%
M35	Powerglide Automatic Transmission	2,621	12.2%
L84	327ci, 360 hp Engine (fuel injection)	2,610	12.1%
898	Genuine Leather Seats	1,114	5.2%
A01	Soft Ray Tinted Glass, all windows	629	2.9%
A02	Soft Ray Tinted Glass, windshield	470	2.2%
P91	6.70x15 Blackwall Tires	412	1.9%
T86	Back-up Lamps	318	1.5%
C60	Air Conditioning	278	1.3%
G91	Special Highway Axle, 3.08:1 Ratio	211	1.0%
Z06	Special Performance Equipment	199	0.9%
N34	Woodgrained Plastic Steering Wheel	130	0.6%
C48	Heater and Defroster Delete	124	0.6%
N03	36-Gallon Fuel Tank (coupe)	63	0.3%
N11	Off-Road Exhaust System	N/A	0.0%
P48	Cast Aluminum Knock-Off Wheels	N/A	0.0%

* - Of Convertible production

1964

RPO#	Description	Quantity	Percent
U69	AM-FM Radio	20,934	94.2%
P92	6.70x15 Whitewall Tires	19,977	89.9%
M20	4-Speed Manual Transmission	19,034	85.6%
G81	Positraction Rear Axle	18,279	82.2%
T86	Back-up Lamps	11,085	49.9%
L75	327ci, 300 hp Engine	10,471	47.1%
L76	327ci, 365 hp Engine	7,171	32.3%
C07	Auxiliary Hardtop (convertible)	7,023	50.4%
A02	Soft Ray Tinted Glass, windshield	6,387	28.7%
A01	Soft Ray Tinted Glass, all windows	6,031	27.1%
J65	Power Brakes, Sintered Metallic	4,780	21.5%
A31	Power Windows	3,706	16.7%
N40	Power Steering	3,126	14.1%
M35	Powerglide Automatic Transmission	2,480	11.2%
G91	Special Highway Axle - 3.08:1 Ratio	2,310	10.4%
J50	Power Brakes	2,270	10.2%
C60	Air Conditioning	1,988	8.9%
N11	Off-Road Exhaust System	1,953	8.8%
N/A	Genuine Leather Seats	1,334	6.0%
L84	327ci, 375 hp Engine (fuel injection)	1,325	6.0%
P48	Cast Aluminum Knock-Off Wheels	806	3.6%
K66	Transistor Ignition System	552	2.5%
P91	6.70x15 Blackwall Tires	372	1.7%
F40	Special Front and Rear Suspension	82	0.4%
C48	Heater and Defroster Delete	60	0.3%
N03	36-Gallon Fuel Tank (coupe)	38	0.2%
J56	Special Sintered Metallic Brake Package	29	0.1%

1965

RPO#	Description	Quantity	Percent
U69	AM-FM Radio	22,113	93.9%
M20	4-Speed Manual Transmission	21,107	89.6%
G81	Positraction Rear Axle	19,965	84.7%
P92	7.75x15 Whitewall Tires	19,300	81.9%
Z01	Comfort and Convenience Group	15,397	65.3%
A01	Soft Ray Tinted Glass, all windows	8,752	37.1%
L75	327ci, 300 hp Engine	8,358	35.5%
C07	Auxiliary Hardtop (convertible)	7,787	50.6%
A02	Soft Ray Tinted Glass, windshield	7,624	32.4%
L76	327ci, 365 hp Engine	5,011	21.3%
L79	327ci, 350 hp Engine	4,716	20.0%
J50	Power Brakes	4,044	17.2%
N36	Telescopic Steering Wheel	3,917	16.6%
A31	Power Windows	3,809	16.2%

RPO#	Description	Quantity	Percent
K66	Transistor Ignition System	3,686	15.6%
N40	Power Steering	3,236	13.7%
N11	Off-Road Exhaust System	2,468	10.5%
C60	Air Conditioning	2,423	10.3%
N32	Teakwood Steering Wheel	2,259	9.6%
L78	396ci, 425 hp Engine	2,157	9.2%
N/A	Genuine Leather Seats	2,128	9.0%
M35	Powerglide Automatic Transmission	2,021	8.6%
G91	Special Highway Axle - 3.08:1 Ratio	1,886	8.0%
P48	Cast Aluminum Knock-Off Wheels	1,116	4.7%
T01	7.75x15 Goldwall Tires	989	4.2%
F40	Special Front and Rear Suspension	975	4.1%
L84	327ci, 375 hp Engine (fuel injection)	771	3.3%
N14	Side Mount Exhaust System	759	3.2%
J61	Drum Brakes (credit)	316	1.3%
P91	7.75x15 Blackwall Tires	168	0.7%
N03	36-Gallon Fuel Tank (coupe)	41	0.2%
C48	Heater and Defroster Delete	39	0.2%

1966

RPO#	Description	Quantity	Percent
U69	AM-FM Radio	26,363	95.1%
G81	Positraction Rear Axle	24,056	86.8%
P92	7.75x15 Whitewall Tires	17,969	64.8%
M21	4-Speed Manual Transmission, close ratio	13,903	50.2%
A01	Soft Ray Tinted Glass, all windows	11,859	42.8%
M20	4-Speed Manual Transmission	10,837	39.1%
A02	Soft Ray Tinted Glass, windshield	9,270	33.4%
C07	Auxiliary Hardtop (convertible)	8,463	47.6%
L79	327ci, 350 hp Engine	7,591	27.4%
K66	Transistor Ignition System	7,146	25.8%
V74	Traffic Hazard Lamp Switch	5,764	20.8%
N40	Power Steering	5,611	20.2%
T01	7.75x15 Goldwall Tires	5,557	20.0%
J50	Power Brakes	5,464	19.7%
L72	427ci, 450 hp/425 hp Engine	5,258	19.0%
L36	427ci, 390 hp Engine	5,116	18.5%
A31	Power Windows	4,562	16.5%
N32	Teakwood Steering Wheel	3,941	14.2%
N36	Telescopic Steering Wheel	3,670	13.2%
N14	Side Mount Exhaust System	3,617	13.0%
C60	Air Conditioning	3,520	12.7%
N11	Off-Road Exhaust System	2,795	10.1%
F41	Special Front and Rear Suspension	2,705	9.8%
M35	Powerglide Automatic Transmission	2,401	8.7%
K19	Air Injection Reactor	2,380	8.6%
N/A	Genuine Leather Seats	2,002	7.2%
P48	Cast Aluminum Knock-Off Wheels	1,194	4.3%
A82	Headrests	1,033	3.7%
J56	Special Heavy Duty Brakes	382	1.4%
N03	36.5-Gallon Fuel Tank (coupes)	66	0.2%
C48	Heater and Defroster Deletion	54	0.2%
A85	Shoulder Belts	37	0.1%
M22	4-Speed Manual Trans close ratio, Heavy Duty	15	0.1%

1967

RPO#	Description	Quantity	Percent
U69	AM-FM Radio	22,193	96.7%
G81	Positraction Rear Axle	20,308	88.5%
P92	7.75x15 Whitewall Tires	13,445	58.6%
A01	Soft Ray Tinted Glass, all windows	11,331	49.4%
M21	4-Speed Manual Transmission, close ratio	11,015	48.0%
M20	4-Speed Manual Transmission	9,157	39.9%
C07	Auxiliary Hardtop (convertible)	6,880	47.7%
A02	Soft Ray Tinted Glass, windshield	6,668	29.1%
L79	327ci, 350 hp Engine	6,375	27.8%
K66	Transistor Ignition System	5,759	25.1%
N40	Power Steering	5,747	25.1%
J50	Power Brakes	4,766	20.8%
QB1	7.75x15 Redline Tires	4,230	18.4%
N14	Side Mount Exhaust System	4,209	18.3%
A31	Power Windows	4,036	17.6%
L36	427ci, 390 hp Engine	3,832	16.7%
C60	Air Conditioning	3,788	16.5%
L71	427ci, 435 hp Engine	3,754	16.4%
K19	Air Injection Reactor	2,573	11.2%
N36	Telescopic Steering Wheel	2,415	10.5%
N11	Off-Road Exhaust System	2,326	10.1%
M35	Powerglide Automatic Transmission	2,324	10.1%
F41	Special Front and Rear Suspension	2,198	9.6%
U15	Speed Warning Indicator	2,108	9.2%
L68	427ci, 400 hp Engine	2,101	9.2%
C08	Vinyl Covering (for Auxiliary Hardtop)	1,966	13.6%
A82	Headrests	1,762	7.7%
N/A	Genuine Leather Seats	1,601	7.0%
A85	Shoulder Belts	1,426	6.2%
N89	Cast Aluminum Bolt-On Wheels	720	3.1%
J56	Special Heavy Duty Brakes	267	1.2%
C48	Heater and Defroster Deletion	35	0.2%
L88	427ci, 430 hp Engine	20	0.1%
M22	4-Speed Manual Trans close ratio, Heavy Duty	20	0.1%
L89	Aluminum Cylinder Heads with L71 Engine	16	0.1%
N03	36-Gallon Fuel Tank (coupe)	2	